Hold Them NEAR

© 2017 by TGS International, a wholly owned subsidiary of Christian Aid Ministries, Berlin, Ohio.

All rights reserved. No part of this book may be used, reproduced, or stored in any retrieval system, in any form or by any means, electronic or mechanical, without written permission from the publisher except for brief quotations embodied in critical articles and reviews.

ISBN: 978-1-943929-70-2

All Scripture quotations are from the King James Version.

This book is a revised, expanded version of the author's 1990 self-published book with the same title.

Front cover photos: Jessica Rose Photography
Back cover photo: Marvin R. Beachy
Photo on back cover is the house the Beachys lived in when the story began.

Published by:
TGS International
P.O. Box 355, Berlin, Ohio 44610 USA
Phone: 330-893-4828
Fax: 330-893-2305
www.tgsinternational.com

TGS001406

CATHERINE BEACHY YODER

The Bible and eyeglasses shown here belonged to Sara Beachy. Sara's babies wore the shoes and booties. The quilt was made by Sara, for the author and the author's sister.

Dedication

This book is dedicated to my mother, Amy, for her tireless encouragement, and to all the Beachys and Hochstetlers who have supported me in countless ways.

We Have This Moment Today

Hold tight to the sound of the music of living,
Happy songs from the laughter of children at play;
Hold my hand as we run
Through the sweet, fragrant meadows,
Making memories of what was today.

Tiny voice that I hear is my little girl calling
For Daddy to hear just what she has to say;
And my little son
Running there by the hillside
May never be quite like today.

Tender words, gentle touch,
and a good cup of coffee,
And someone who loves me and wants me to stay;

Hold them near
while they're here

And don't wait for tomorrow
To look back and wish for today.

We have this moment to hold in our hands
And to touch as it slips through
our fingers like sand.
Yesterday's gone and
tomorrow may never come,
But we have this moment today.[1]

---

[1] "We Have This Moment Today." Words by Gloria Gaither. Music by William J. Gaither. © Copyright 1975 by William J. Gaither. All rights reserved. Used by permission. Emphasis added.

Preface

Grandmas tell stories.

My grandma used to tell stories about her boys and all the mischief they got into when they were young. She would shake her head and laugh. And she thanked God they had survived! She would chat for hours in Pennsylvania Dutch with her sisters, the stories and laughter ringing over the crowded confusion of children and grandchildren. She told me stories about her old dishes, some of which had been brought from France when our ancestors came to America on a ship. She told me the family legend that some of our ancestors were chosen as Napoleon's bodyguards because, like him, they were very short. But she never told me much about the story you are about to read.

I was only sixteen when Grandma died. I took for

granted that she was a happy woman, a pillar of spiritual strength in her church and family. Only now, looking back, do I fully appreciate the grace of God in her life. I see how God used tragedies to transform a carefree young woman into an example of tenacious trust in Him.

This grandma-story is true. I've reconstructed the details that time has blurred, but the facts remain. A book like this is an undertaking by the entire family. Thank you to all those who answered questions, shared memories, gave encouragement, and prayed. Thanks especially to Margaret (Beachy) Miller, who assisted with proofreading.

My paternal grandparents, Noah and Sara (Hochstetler) Beachy, would not have wanted to be lifted up as heroes, but would have wanted God to be glorified through their story. If God becomes more real to you through this book, if you hold your loved ones a little closer, if you can trust Him more fully, our prayers are answered.

"But the mercy of the LORD is from everlasting to everlasting upon them that fear him, and his righteousness unto children's children" (Psalm 103:17).

—Catherine (Beachy) Yoder, 2016

Chapter 1

Happiness ran high.

"When are we going to Dawdy's?[1] When are we going to Dawdy's?" Five-year-old Mary Lou hopped around the living room, giddy with happiness.

"I'm taking my dolly," little sister Judy said. "But where is my dolly's diaper bag?"

"Children, children, settle down! The driver will be here soon. Do you all have coats and gloves?" Sara glanced around the living room, automatically counting five little heads, diaper bags, suitcases. *I'm looking forward to spending Christmas with my parents,* she thought, *but this trip feels like a big undertaking.*

Noah entered the house, stomping snow off his boots.

---

[1] "Dawdy" is a Pennsylvania Dutch term for "Grandpa."

"The chores are done. Are you ready, Sara?" Taking off his straw hat, he raked his fingers through thick black hair before brushing the snow from his bushy beard.

"I hope I remembered everything," Sara said. "I can hardly wait to see everyone again! Some of my sisters haven't even seen the baby yet." Sara searched her husband's face, but his eyes didn't meet hers. His thoughts were elsewhere. *I know we are committed to each other no matter what, but sometimes I don't think he really understands me. Does he know how much this trip means to me? We got married so young and too quickly. Now, with five children, we hardly have time to talk with each other.*

"Here comes the car!" Six-year-old Marvin's announcement from his post at the front window brought Sara's attention back to the present.

In a flurry of activity, the men packed the luggage in the trunk, and the children piled into the spacious old sedan. Noah and Marvin shared the front seat with the driver, while Sara settled in the back with the three little girls and baby Henry. Anticipation bubbled inside her as she smiled at the excited children. Sara patted Barbara Jean's curly blond hair. The toddler had no idea how long this trip would take, but she caught the other children's exhilaration and bounced on the seat beside her mother. Rarely did these children get to make the two-hundred-mile trip from their home in Plain City, Ohio, to Nappanee, Indiana.

"So when do you think the gas rationing will end?" Noah started the conversation with the driver.

"It won't be long, now that the war is over, I'm sure. I didn't have any problems getting enough coupons for this trip," the driver said. "The time can't come too soon for me, I will tell you that. And I am tired of driving only thirty-five miles an hour!"

The miles rumbled by. Snowy little towns had been decked out for this Christmas of 1945, as the economy emerged from the tensions and fears of the Great Depression and World War II. *Maybe this season will truly be a time of peace on earth,* Sara mused, reflecting on the troubled times they had come through.

Gradually the children's excitement simmered down, and they fell asleep. Sara leaned her head against the seat back. *Thank you, Lord, for my blessings*, she prayed silently. *Five healthy children, enough money to pay the bills, a hardworking husband, and now a chance to see my family again. Thank you!*

When the family arrived at their destination, Henry and Mary Hochstetler welcomed Noah, Sara, and the children with hugs and beaming smiles. "How's my new little Henry?" Short and cheery, Dawdy wrinkled his nose to make the baby chuckle. "You look just like your big brother! Marvin, are you teaching him to do chores yet?" Fondly Dawdy patted Marvin's shoulder. "You grew since the last time I saw you! You need to come out and see what I've been building in the shop."

The welcoming party kept expanding. Sara's sister Susie, with baby Glenn on her hip, bustled in from her house next door. Noah and Sara's older children started playing with the other cousins. Aunt Wilma entertained the nieces, while Uncle Joni[2] pulled Marvin and John Henry aside. "Hey, boys, come up to my room. I want to show you something."

Eagerly the six-year-olds followed him. Joni had the most interesting toys! This time it was a wind-up tractor with caterpillar treads. Joni was twenty-five, but he still loved playing with his nephews and knew what would interest them. He set up blocks for the toy tractor to crawl over. Enthralled, Marvin begged, "May I wind it up? Please?"

"I guess, but be careful," Joni said. The boys played for hours.

---

[2] Pronounced JOH-nee.

The next day Sara watched the family commotion multiply as her two married brothers and the three married sisters with their fifteen children came to celebrate Christmas. She pulled the rocking chair into the kitchen to nurse Henry. "I don't want to miss out on anything!" Sara explained. How she had missed those boisterous Pennsylvania Dutch sister conversations!

"Mom, that turkey and dressing smell delicious!" Sara said, savoring the aroma. "I wish I could help more, but Henry is being so fussy."

"You just take care of that baby." Mary, her face flushed from working over the hot stove, turned to smile at her fourth daughter. "We're so glad you could finally come out to visit. Letters are just not the same as seeing all of you."

"Barbara Jean is such a daddy's girl, isn't she?" Sara's sister Barbara asked, looking wistfully toward her namesake, who clung to her father in the living room. "After fifteen years I sure wish we could have children of our own! But it doesn't seem to be God's will."

"I know exactly how you feel," Christena, another sister, said. "It sure is fun to see all these little ones running around."

"Well, I guess *somebody* needs their hands free to

cook!" Barbara chuckled wryly as she went back to stirring the potato salad.

I love my family, thought Sara, still cradling Henry. *I love their positive attitudes. We were raised to trust God, even in difficult times. After all, God knows best. Why fuss about less than ideal circumstances?* Sara's faith stood like a tender sapling, unaccustomed to harsh winds. Would it weather the storms ahead?

Chapter

The baby slept.

Mary Lou wearily pushed back a strand of dark hair. She rose cautiously from the rocker and laid baby Henry on the couch. "Judy, he's finally sleeping," she whispered to her younger sister.

"Let's go tell Mommy!" Judy's blue eyes sparkled with excitement. "Mommy will be so glad! She said he didn't sleep much last night."

Hand in hand, the girls hurried through the house's dim interior. Drawn shades at the windows blocked the morning sunlight. Finding their coats, Mary Lou and Judy dressed quickly for the January cold and then ran across the snowy lawn to the wash line.

Sara smiled as she saw the girls coming. Her "little

helpers," she called them. *With five children under seven years old, the work certainly piles up!* she mused. The wind tugged at the dark coat wrapped around her slight form, and the cold stung her fingers as she pinned up the last diaper. *They must have put Henry to sleep. He's been crying so much all weekend! I wonder what's wrong with him. The doctor thought it was indigestion, but his suggestion to give soda water hasn't helped much. I hope keeping the house dark helps him sleep all morning.*

"Mommy, he's sleeping!" Judy said.

"Good for you, girls! I'm done here, so I'll come in and check on him. Mary Lou, why don't you carry the basket for me?"

The trio walked toward the old farmhouse. All around them, the peaceful countryside, clad in snow, sparkled in the winter sun. Even though the day was only beginning, Sara could feel the weariness in her bones. The nighttime interruptions of the past three months since Henry's birth had taken their toll. *God, give me the strength for another Monday,* she prayed silently.

They walked up the steps and entered the dimness of the house. As the three crossed the room to the worn couch, Sara intuitively stiffened. "Something's wrong here," she said, almost to herself. Just then the baby threw his tiny arms into the air and drew a raspy breath. Then he lay still.

Sara's heart lurched. Her mind reeled, refusing to believe what she knew to be true. Her baby was gone.

Judy's wide-eyed gaze traveled from the still form on the couch to her mother's frozen face. "Mommy! MOMMY!" she shrieked, grabbing Sara's hand. "What's wrong?"

"He ... died." Sara's breathless words broke the news to the girls. Numb with shock, she picked up the body of her darling baby and cradled him to herself. His lifeless form lay limp as a rag doll in her arms. Jumbled thoughts spun through her tired brain: *Henry's gone ... what made him die? ... must tell Noah ... be brave for the girls ... turn off the washing machine ... check on Barbara Jean ... my baby is dead ... could I have done something for him?* Surges of grief welled up inside and tears spilled down her cheeks.

Mary Lou and Judy stood transfixed next to the quiet couch. Sara raised her weary gaze to see two pairs of eyes searching her face. She could read the fear and bewilderment on their faces. *Perhaps they wonder if it is their fault that Henry died. They probably thought only animals and old people die.* Forcing her anguish aside, Sara put on her habitual calm demeanor. *My children need me. My grief will have to wait.* Gently she laid down the inert form and turned to hug the girls. *How dearly I love the children I still have!* she realized. Turning from the sofa, she said, "Let's go check on Barbara Jean and then find Dad and Marvin."

They walked over to Barbara Jean's bed. The twenty-one-month-old was sleeping soundly, her golden curls scattered over the pillow. A faint flush gave her cheeks a rosy glow. *Such a perfect child,* Sara thought indulgently. Then she jerked back to reality. *Barbara Jean is fine. Henry is gone. I have to break the news to Noah somehow. What will he say? Will he think it was my fault?* Sara squeezed back tears and forced herself to walk calmly out the door.

Still bundled up, the three trudged to the barn. Inside, the warm, pungent odor of horses and hay, cows and feed greeted them. Tall, broad-shouldered Noah and six-year-old Marvin were doing chores together. At the sound of the door, they turned. Sara's pale face forewarned Noah that she brought bad news. "What's wrong?" he asked brusquely.

Sara looked past his fierce black beard into his caring blue eyes. *Bluntness is best,* she decided. "You need to come to the house. Henry just died." There, she said it.

She had kept her voice flat, without emotion. She had to keep a hold on herself.

"What happened?" Noah's eyes widened with shock. Marvin's face froze, his pitchfork suddenly still beside his father's.

Sara grasped her husband's arm and poured out the story. "I asked the girls to take turns rocking him while I hung out the laundry. After a while they came and told me he was sleeping. I went in to check on him, and just then he threw his hands into the air and was gone!"

"Oh, Sara, no!" Noah breathed. "Are you sure? He didn't seem that sick!" Mechanically he latched the gate and grabbed his hat as he ran toward the house. In stunned silence, the rest of the family hurried after him out of the warm barn. Seeing the motionless body on the couch broke their reserves; the tears flowed. Clinging together, parents and children wept. The baby had been such a precious part of their family!

Noah grieved for Henry. He loved his girls, but there was something special about his sons. He bit his lip to hold back the sobs.

Scared and bewildered, Mary Lou and Judy tried to comprehend what had happened. Their childish minds could scarcely grasp the grim finality of death.

No longer would they be able to cuddle their sweet little brother.

Marvin stared, wide-eyed. He knew Henry had been sick, but he had no idea death lurked so near. His sturdy young frame shook with sobs.

Sara squeezed Marvin's hand through her own pain. She knew how delighted he had been at the thought of a younger brother to work beside him on the farm. Silently she cried out to God in her anguish. *God, I can't believe this happened! Why? Why? We loved him so much! And our other children . . . How do we help them through this? Oh, Lord, we need your help! Please give us the strength we need right now!*

Noah awkwardly wiped tears from his cheeks and looked helplessly at Sara. "What do we do first?" he asked, still stunned with shock.

"We need to make lots of phone calls, I guess. First the Ferguson Funeral Home, of course. Then call your folks, and get a message to my folks."

"Mama, Mama!" Barbara Jean's small feet pattered across the floor. Her newly-awakened smile always brought a special thrill to her mother. Sara reached to pick her up. "Mama cry?" Barbara Jean's chubby hand patted Sara's damp cheek.

"Honey, Henry just died, so Mommy's sad." Of course the child couldn't understand, but in her own charming way she could soothe a bit of the hurt. Sara hugged her tightly. The agony of losing her baby made her want to love her remaining children all the more.

Still in a daze, Noah headed for the phone. The church they attended allowed telephones in rental houses like theirs. Watching him, Sara thought, *At a time like this, I'm glad we have a phone. He's probably relieved he doesn't have to face anyone just yet.*

Noah's younger brother answered the phone. Noah's parents, Eli C. and Mary Ann Beachy, weren't home. Noah's voice sounded strained. "Neil, could you give the folks a message right away? You know Henry's been sick all weekend? Well, he just died . . ."

Sara stood close to Noah as he called the operator again, this time to place a call to Nappanee, Indiana. Her thoughts went back to their last visit with her family. *Was that only three weeks ago? What a happy time it had been!*

The call went through. "Hello? Hello, this is Noah Beachy from Plain City, Ohio, calling. Could you get a message to your neighbors, Henry and Mary Hochstetler, right away? Our baby, Henry, which is their grandson, just died . . ."

Soon Noah's parents drove up the long lane. They had been in the midst of butchering at Alvin Kramer's farm a few miles away, but had dropped their work immediately to go comfort their son and his family. "Oh, Noah, Sara, what happened?" Mary Ann asked, her eyes brimming with tears. Sara just shook her head and reached out for a hug. She had no words and no answers.

Behind them came Mr. Ferguson, the undertaker, his face stolid below his crop of graying hair. Sara watched him soberly as he walked to the couch. *I wonder how many babies he has buried over the years,* she thought. *And it's such a miserable time of year to have a funeral!*

Noah helped Mr. Ferguson get the body ready to move, then drew Sara aside. "Dad could take me to Abe Miller's to order a casket. Do you think we'd want the funeral on Wednesday? We'll stop by your sister Christena's and also let the bishop know. You'll be all right since Mom's here, won't you?"

Silently Sara nodded. She felt God's strength holding her up, giving her a calmness not her own. The verse she had underlined in her Bible recently took on new meaning for her: "The LORD is nigh unto them that are of a broken heart" (Psalm 34:18).

"I'll be okay," she told Noah, her voice nearly steady.

As Noah and his father drove down the road, Eli allowed his son time for introspection. Finally Noah voiced his troubled thoughts. "I know we don't have much money, but I should have called the doctor out to the house. How could he tell over the phone that the baby just had a stomachache? Maybe Henry's death is my fault."

"You're doing the best you know in raising your family," Eli comforted. "Now you have to commit this situation to God and trust Him." Noah sighed, his heart still heavy.

Having completed their errands, Noah and Eli drove back up the long driveway that led to Noah and Sara's home. Already a row of buggies lined the fence. News spread rapidly in this small Ohio community.

Inside the house Noah found a subdued bustle of activity. Neighbors and friends surrounded Sara.

"I brought a casserole for dinner. Should I put it in the oven?"

"Let me start cleaning the front room. Where are your cleaning rags?"

"Here's some white fabric I had on hand. Would it be okay for a burial gown? I can sew it up for you."

"Do you have any more laundry to do? I'll be glad to finish it up."

"Children, come listen to this story." The children gathered around a thoughtful neighbor, who read them a story to keep them occupied.

Funeral preparations were underway.

· · · · · · · · · ·

"What is that smell?" Mary Lou stood beside her mother, looking at the cotton-wrapped form of her baby brother. In keeping with Amish tradition, Mr. Ferguson had brought the body back to the house where Sara would dress it in a simple white burial gown.

"It stinks!" Marvin and Judy agreed.

Sara breathed deeply. That sickly-sweet embalming odor permeated the whole house, reminding her with every breath she took that life would never be the same again. How she hated that smell!

Sara walked through the days in a blur. *How can this be happening? My baby is dead!* People, people, people filled the house at all hours. They showed their love by taking care of all the details: serving the food, organizing the viewing, shedding tears, and drying them.

"Sara!" A familiar voice pierced her fog of grief.

"Oh, Susie..." Sara stumbled toward her sister. Tears flowed freely as they embraced. Sara looked around at the whole circle of her family—parents and siblings who had traveled from Indiana to comfort the grief-stricken family. *These are my people.* Their presence soothed her heart.

The funeral took place on Wednesday at their neighbor Roy Miller's home, since their house was larger than Noah's. In spite of the cold weather, the house was filled with the young couple's friends.

It was only a short trip from the Miller house to the cemetery after the service. Marvin, Mary Lou, and Judy huddled close to their parents in a corner of the snowy graveyard. The brown dirt piled beside the grave blotched an ugly stain on the pristine whiteness.

The children listened solemnly to the black-clad bishop as his voice led out in the familiar German:

> *Gute Nacht, ihr meine Lieben;*
> *Gute Nacht, ihr Herzensfreund;*
> *Gute Nacht, die sich betrüben,*
> *Und aus Lieb für mich jetzt weint...*

Many voices joined in song, repeating the lines from the ten-verse poem as men began to shovel dirt over the simple casket. Sara heard the long benediction through a haze of despair.

Someday, she assumed, those words would comfort her, but not yet.

> Good night to my beloved;
> Good night, my heartfelt friends;
> Good night to those who sorrow
> And who weep because of love for me.
>
> Even though I depart from you,
> And you lay my body in the grave,
> It will rise again,
> And I will see you eternally.
>
> Because my troubles now have ended,
> For this my beloved parents are glad,
> Thank God for working out His love,
> And be no more burdened with sorrow for me.
>
> Father, Mother, so good night,
> Remember what God does is done well;
> Even though your hearts do sorrow,

He loves me and you as well.[1]

"Thank God for working out His love"? I don't feel His love right now, Sara thought. The biting cold that made her fingers and toes tingle seemed to have numbed her heart as well.

---

[1] Translated by Daniel Bontrager from *Liedersammlung* (Amish German hymnal).

Chapter

Thursday was empty.

Disconsolately the children wandered through the house. Barbara Jean often wiped her runny nose on Sara's worn apron. In spite of their own listlessness, the older girls tried to keep the toddler amused. Marvin escaped the gloomy atmosphere by spending time outside or in the barn with his dad. Sara mourned silently as she went on with her work. Her arms felt so empty, and her ears still strained to catch the familiar cry of her baby.

Her thoughts turned often to Psalm 91:1–2. *"He that dwelleth in the secret place of the most High shall abide under the shadow of the Almighty. I will say of the LORD, He is my refuge and my fortress: my God; in him will*

I trust." I have to trust God in this. Somehow, Henry's death must have been the Lord's will. Even though I don't understand it, He will give me the strength to go on. Lord, hide me in your shadow! Be my refuge! I do trust you.

So Sara went on. She grieved with Noah, answered Marvin's questions, and kept the girls' hair neatly braided. When Sunday came, they all donned their best clothes and attended church services as usual.

The orderly service brought a measure of peace to Sara's troubled heart. The plainly dressed women with their crisp white coverings and aprons and openly sympathetic faces were so dear to her!

Across the room she watched Noah find a spot on the backless bench next to Melvin Miller, who was visiting from a neighboring district that day. Noah's face had grown some new wrinkles through the sorrow of the past week. Sara thanked God that her husband had good friends like Melvin. *I hope Noah has a chance to share his heart with Melvin today,* she thought. *It's hard for him to open up about his grief.*

"*O Gott Vater, wir loben dich . . .*" (O God Father, we praise you . . .) Voices in unison carried the familiar tune of the *Loblied*, the second hymn sung at the beginning of every Amish church service. Slowly Sara loosened the tense rein she had kept on her emotions all week. Quiet tears trickled down her cheeks as the music surrounded her. Hungry for refreshment, she drank in the minister's words. "I am the resurrection, and the life: he that believeth in me, though he were dead, yet shall he live" (John 11:25).

Sara shifted the weight of sleeping Barbara Jean from one arm to the other. *I wonder what Henry is experiencing right now, safe and healthy forever in heaven.* She pictured her precious baby, cradled in the arms of Jesus, smiling up into His face. Her grief would take time to heal, but the sharpness of its sting had already begun to soften. Like her baby, she too was finding peace and rest in Jesus' arms.

After church, friends surrounded Sara again with condolences. "At least you still have Barbara Jean," one of the women told her.

"She is so pretty!" another said.

Sara gazed down at her little daughter. "It will be hard to teach her humility, I'm afraid," she said. Even to her close friends, Sara could not admit her deep feelings about this child. In fact, Sara was almost afraid to take Barbara Jean to town for fear the golden-haired charmer would be kidnapped. Last summer one time

Barbara Jean's bonnet had blown off, and an "English"[1] man ran to catch it. When he returned, he exclaimed over and over about how beautiful the child was. But Barbara Jean stood out in other ways besides her physical appearance. None of Sara's other children had ever toilet-trained themselves, or wiped their own noses, or ate without making a mess, or obeyed without needing a spanking!

"Remember the morning she was born?" Sara's sister Christena had joined the conversation. Her face brightened when she heard Sara talking about something other than Henry's death. "It was a frosty April morning, and each twig and blade of grass was sparkling white. I came over while Noah went for the doctor. By the time the doctor arrived, the excitement was all over. Barbara Jean was cute even then!"

"Yes, we're thankful for such a sweet girl," Sara said, "but I still miss my baby."

* * * * * * * * * *

"Noah, I'm worried about Barbara Jean."

---

[1] Many Amish people use the term "English" to refer to a non-Amish person.

"What's the matter with her?"

"She's just been coughing and coughing. Listen to her breathing. I think she's seriously sick."

"Do you think I should call out the doctor?"

"Please do. I don't want to take any risks."

Noah turned to the phone, his hands shaking. Another sick child! Memories of the anguish of Henry's recent death came over him in a rush. On Monday after they had taken Barbara Jean to the doctor, she had seemed to be getting better. Now her condition had worsened.

Sara paced the floor, bouncing Barbara Jean gently as Noah dialed. She had noticed that Barbara Jean had been eating less since her bout with the flu in December, but the toddler had been quiet and reasonably happy despite the disrupted routine of the past week. On the day of Henry's funeral, Barbara Jean did have a cold, so Sara had left her in the house with friends instead of taking her to the cemetery. Still, Barbara Jean had acted cheerful. She had waved and said goodbye to almost everyone there. Now the little girl seemed flushed, feverish, and discontent. And the weather was dreadful, with a cold wind driving icy snowflakes through the Friday twilight.

"Hello, Doctor, Noah Beachy calling from Plain City. If you remember, we brought in our daughter, Barbara Jean, on Monday. Today she still seems to have a fever, and now she is having a hard time breathing. Would you be able to come out and look at her?"

Mary Lou and Judy came into the room, overhearing the words. Their faces looked scared. They knew Barbara Jean must be really sick because their parents didn't call the doctor often. That day Sara hadn't allowed Barbara Jean outside, but the toddler had felt well enough to crawl up on the sewing machine and wave to her mother when she went out to do chores. After that she had just whimpered until her parents came back in.

"What did he say?" Sara's anxious eyes sought Noah's as he finished the conversation. She noted the worry lines that creased his forehead.

"He'll be right out."

"Could you make the other children some sandwiches while I rock Barbara Jean?" Sara asked. "I know they're hungry."

"I'll fry up some cheese sandwiches right away," Noah said. Soon the smell of grilled cheese eased the girls' worry and enticed Marvin into the room. They had just started their hasty meal when the doctor arrived.

"Nasty weather," he said, closing the porch door behind him. "So, where's my patient?"

Noah led him into the bedroom, explaining his daughter's symptoms as he went.

The doctor wasted no time. As he listened with the stethoscope, his brow furrowed. "I don't like the sound of that breathing. I think you should take her to Children's Hospital in Columbus right away. It could be pneumonia, and she would be better off there."

Fear registered in Sara's brown eyes. *Children's Hospital? None of us ever had to go there. All five of my children were born at home with no trouble. Even last summer when Marvin got so sick from gas fumes, we never took him to the hospital.*

The picture of that day was etched in Sara's memory. Her young musician was standing on the cultivator hitched to the Farmall F-20 and singing into the tractor's gas tank. "I like the way it sounds," he said. Marvin had sung until he passed out before Noah found him and carried him back to the house. When Marvin had regained consciousness, he had been so surprised to find himself on the porch.

They had all laughed afterward, when they knew he

was okay. But now the doctor was saying Barbara Jean needed to go to the hospital!

"Okay, let's go," Noah announced firmly. "I'll call a driver, and we'll drop the children off at Roy's place."

With shaking, desperate fingers, Sara started packing an overnight bag. *What do I need to take? I wonder how long we'll be there. I can't leave Barbara Jean there alone! Twenty-five miles is just too far from home. Oh, God, please help me!* Immediately Sara felt a peace settle over her spirit. Quickly she finished the task. Casting an anxious glance at the weather outside, she wrapped Barbara Jean in several blankets even though the toddler was feverish. *That snow looks threatening. I'm not taking any chances.* By the time the driver arrived, they were ready to head to Columbus.

Soon they reached the city. Brightly lit store windows flashed by. No one spoke. Rasping coughs reminded them all of the seriousness of their errand. Silent prayers went up from Noah and Sara as they turned in at the imposing brick hospital in the middle of town.

Noah carried Barbara Jean through the glass doors into the emergency room. The smell of hospital antiseptic, the sight of women pacing the floor while men smoked nervously, and the sound of doctors being summoned on the intercom unnerved him. Impatiently he answered the receptionist's questions. *I know how he feels,* thought Sara. *He wishes they would just hurry and look at Barbara Jean.* Finally an orderly came and wheeled the little girl away to be examined.

"We'll need to have you sign this form, Mr. Beachy." The nurse pushed a half-sheet of paper toward him. "They can't treat her until you do."

Noah and Sara read the brief document together.

PERMISSION FOR OPERATION
Date: January 25, 1946
Permission is hereby granted to the authorities of Children's Hospital, Columbus, Ohio, for such procedures as may be necessary in the case of <u>Barbara Jean Beachy</u> for any medical and surgical procedures including the giving of anesthetics, which may be necessary. We will not hold the hospital responsible in case any contagious disease is contracted.
WITNESS: [signed] Ferne M. Holmes, R.N.
SIGNED: _____

Grimly, Noah signed it.

"Can we go in with the baby?" Sara asked timidly.

"No, you'd better wait out here. They should be out before long."

The minutes dragged by. Their driver had settled down with a magazine, waiting to see whether the couple would need a ride home. Noah fidgeted in his chair, crossing his legs and tapping his foot. Sara prayed quietly. *What are they finding out?* she wondered.

Stretcher wheels rattled in the hall. Noah and Sara looked up quickly. Was it Barbara Jean? The golden hair confirmed it. Would they have to keep her here overnight?

Noah and Sara stood up to meet the emergency room physician, who, to their surprise, was a woman.

"I think she has pneumonia in the left lung."

Continuing, Dr. Leech answered their unspoken question. "We'll put her in isolation on the second floor. We've given her some sulfides and taken an X-ray. Follow us up to her room."

Sara held the baby's dimpled hand all the way up to her room. She could feel the rapid pulse, and she noted with dismay a tinge of blue around Barbara Jean's lips in her otherwise pale face. *Will she be okay? I've often felt that this child is too good to keep, too precious to remain on this sinful earth. Is she going to die? Pneumonia isn't really serious, is it?* Sara clenched her teeth to keep from crying out.

When they got to Room 224, Dr. Leech sprang into action, ordering an oxygen tent, an IV, and medication. "You might as well go home," she told the couple. "Call us in the morning to get a report."

Sara shot a pleading look at Noah. "We don't want to go," he said firmly. "We're prepared to spend the night. We don't want to leave Barbara Jean."

"The hospital has no place for parents to stay," the doctor snapped, her voice tired. "She will be fine. Now go on home and get some rest."

"But . . ."

The doctor sighed impatiently. "We'll let you know if you're needed."

Wordlessly Noah and Sara kissed the baby and walked out of the room. Behind them they heard Barbara Jean's restless crying. *Why can't we stay? We wouldn't be any trouble!* Even from the sidewalk outside, Sara could hear her daughter's cries. Her mother-heart ached.

"What's the matter with that doctor?" Noah slammed the car door. "Why couldn't we stay?" He kept muttering his opinions as the driver sighed sympathetically and started the car. Sara wept quietly in the back seat. Disappointment and anxiety overwhelmed her. Every mile took her farther from the place she longed to be.

Fortunately the three older children were sleeping when their parents picked them up, so no explanations had to be made. At home, Sara went through the motions of going to bed, but with every breath she petitioned God silently, *Please take care of my baby. Please, please.* The couple spoke little. Sara longed to share her fears with her husband, to seek God's comfort together, but Noah seemed locked in a silent cell of sorrow and anger. Never had Sara felt so helpless and alone. With a heavy heart, she settled down for a restless night.

Chapter

"Her condition's unchanged."

The brief phone report from the hospital did little to alleviate the worry in Sara's heart. Mechanically she added to the postcard she was writing to her sister Barbara.

Plain City, Ohio
Dear Sister,
Greetings in Jesus' holy name.

How are you folks? Hope fine. I am just writing a few lines to let you know we took Barbara Jean to the hospital last night for pneumonia. They didn't allow us to stay there. Sure was hard to leave her.

We had taken her to the doc. on Monday. She got better, but then on Thursday she got worse again. The doc. was out yesterday and said we should take her to the hospital as soon as possible, so we did. We want to call the hospital this morning.

(Later) Report on Barbara this morning is unchanged. Not better nor worse. She had 101.6 fever last night.

Best wishes,
Noah, Sara, and family

I drop a card Monday again.[1]

"Marvin, please run this out to the mailbox for me." Sara pasted on the one-cent stamp.

"But, Mom, it's cold, and the lane is so long!"

"I know, but I want this mailed today so my family finds out about Barbara Jean."

"Well, all right."

Sara continued with her Saturday work, but anxiety nagged at her mind. *Lord, please be with my little girl!* she prayed over and over. She tried to release her fear

---

[1] All letters and diary entries quoted are authentic. Minor spelling and sentence structure changes have been made for clarity.

to God, but she still could not stop worrying. Finally she could stand it no longer. She grabbed her coat and hurried out to the barn.

"Noah, how soon can we go down to Columbus? I just can't bear not being with Barbara Jean!"

"I know what you mean! I'm feeling the same way." Noah rubbed his forehead. "I've done the work that needed to be done today, so I'll come in, call a driver, and clean up. Maybe you can get the children ready to go to the neighbors'."

As Noah and Sara prepared to leave, the phone rang. "Columbus Children's Hospital calling. Is this Noah Beachy?"

"Yes."

"The doctor said you should come down to be with your daughter, Barbara Jean. She's a very sick little girl, and she seems to be getting worse."

"We'll be right down."

Sara knew without asking what the message had been. *Oh, God, please help the doctors with Barbara Jean right now. Be close to her, and help our driver to hurry.* Outwardly Sara stayed calm for the sake of the other children, but inside uneasiness gripped her.

In a short time Noah and Sara found themselves

in a small hospital waiting room on the second floor. Although they had made their presence known, no hospital personnel seemed to have any information for them. They sat and waited.

The hours dragged on. What was happening? Pacing didn't help; reading didn't help. Their prayers felt like words going in circles. They wanted to know about their little girl!

Afternoon wore away to twilight. Suppertime came and passed; neither of them felt hungry. Anxiety continued to gnaw at them.

"I've had all of this I'm going to take!" Noah stood abruptly. "Somebody must know how she is!"

Noah went into the hall and stopped a nurse making her rounds. "I'm Barbara Jean Beachy's father, and I want to see her. Where is she?"

Startled, the nurse tried to evade the question. "Hasn't the doctor been in to see you?"

"No."

"I'll get him." The nurse edged away.

Finally the doctor entered the quiet waiting room. "I'm sorry, but your daughter expired this afternoon. The body is in the morgue waiting to be identified."

The color drained from Sara's face. *Barbara Jean?*

In the morgue? No! It can't be! Tears seemed to choke her. *They didn't tell us! They didn't let us see her, and now she's dead!* Sobs convulsed her small frame. Their precious angel-daughter had been snatched away.

Noah's mouth dropped open in shock. Tears filled his eyes. He reached for Sara's hand and pulled her from the chair. Wordlessly they followed the doctor down to the morgue, where he left them with a receptionist. "She will take care of all the details," he assured them as he walked out.

"Name?" she asked impersonally.

"Noah Beachy. Here to identify our little girl."

"Come this way."

The nauseating smell of the morgue struck them like a blow. On a brightly-lit table they saw Barbara Jean—composed and peaceful, with a slight smile on her face. Her flaxen hair, loose and disheveled, showed the restlessness of her final hours.

Spasms of grief shook the couple as they stared death in the face. Irreversible. The earthly end.

Finally, grudgingly, they accepted the fact. Barbara Jean was dead. But why? How could this possibly be God's will?

Their prolonged silence stirred the secretary to action.

"What funeral home would you like me to contact?"

"Ferguson Funeral Home in Plain City. When did she die, anyway? Why didn't anyone tell us until now?" Agonized questions burned on Noah's lips.

"They brought her down about three this afternoon. I guess the doctor thought you weren't here. If nobody would have claimed the body soon, they would have cremated it."

"But we were here almost all day!"

"I'm sorry, but I have nothing to do with that part of it." She spun on her heel and picked up the phone.

"Oh, Noah, how are we going to tell the children?" Tears started again in Sara's eyes.

"We'd better just call and see if one of the neighbor girls can take them home and put them to bed. I don't want someone else to tell them. Then we will have to explain it all to them when we get home." Noah turned away from the still form. Sara had never seen his face so haggard.

The couple spent ninety cents to send a telegram with the bitter news to Sara's family in Indiana. Then they sat down to await Ferguson's hearse. Weariness and spent emotions had drained all their energy.

It was almost midnight by the time they got home,

accompanied by the memory of that silent body. Quietly they checked on the sleeping children. They couldn't bear to wake them to tell the sad story. Morning would be soon enough.

Sara dreaded the next day.

• • • • • • • • •

A deep sadness prevailed in the house at the end of the long lane. Marvin, Mary Lou, and Judy wandered about in a daze. Mary Lou voiced what all the children felt. "Mommy, Barbara Jean was so good—almost perfect! And she wasn't that sick. Why did she die? Are the rest of us going to die too?"

The news stunned the community. Noah and Sara had lost another child? Church was held only every other Sunday, and this Sunday their district had no service, but visiting families spread the word. Such a short time after the first death! The hearts of their friends ached.

Several families stopped by to offer sympathy and encouragement, but the cold made it difficult for many of their friends to make the buggy ride to the east edge of the settlement where Noah and Sara lived. The newspapers were calling this the coldest wave of the season, with temperatures dropping near zero. Noah's parents drove over with his sister Betty, his brother John, and John's wife Miriam. John, an ordained Mennonite minister, read the familiar words of John 14 to the grieving family.

"Let not your heart be troubled: ye believe in God, believe also in me. In my Father's house are many mansions: if it were not so, I would have told you. I go to prepare a place for you. . . ." (verses 1–2).

Numbly Sara listened to the words. She knew they were true, but she was bruised and aching. *Why, why?* she cried inwardly, as the pain burned within her. *And the way my little girl died!* Sara had seen the bruises where they had strapped down Barbara Jean, and she feared the last hours had been full of agony. *Why should a child have to suffer like that?* The frustration of having been told to leave when her daughter most needed a mother's comforting closeness tormented her. Sara also felt guilty. *Maybe this is my fault. Maybe my babies' deaths are a punishment for my sins in the past, for the sinful choices I made as a teenager . . .*

Sara looked over to see Noah listening to the Scripture while silent tears rolled down into his beard. Last week's loss had been difficult, but now their grief had multiplied. Sara knew Barbara Jean's niche in Noah's heart would never be filled, no matter how many other children they had. What could replace that cheerful giggle, that trusting hand in his? The aching tightness in her throat refused to go away.

". . . And if I go and prepare a place for you, I will come again, and receive you unto myself; that where I am, there ye may be also" (John 14:3).

The promises soothed her sore heart. God had not forsaken her! Somehow she must believe; she must trust. Sara felt the piercing sharpness of her loss, but she reached toward God in total trust. God would hold her in His arms.

Once again the drafty, unadorned farmhouse filled with activity. Once again Sara drew on God's help to care for the three remaining children and work through the details of the funeral. Once again Sara's family paid the fifty dollars to hire a driver and travel from Indiana to share their grief. Once again, each breath was steeped in that deathly embalming smell.

Wednesday morning dawned clear and cold. Roy Miller's house overflowed with people. The young girls who had played with Barbara Jean after church kept glancing at the open casket, crying silently. Barbara Jean had been one of their favorite little people, and they could hardly believe she was gone. Somber-faced relatives and friends mingled quietly, still in various stages of disbelief. Many people lost one child, but to lose two in twelve days? That was unimaginable!

Sara sat motionless on the hard wooden bench at the front of the room with her family. The rapid changes, the emotional draining of the last two weeks were taking their toll. The singing and sermons passed through her consciousness like a blur.

The bishop's words penetrated every corner of the packed room. "We've come today to share the grief of Noah and Sara in this difficult time. It's easy to ask why God would let something like this happen. But God is beyond our understanding. His ways are not like our ways. His thoughts are far beyond our thoughts.

"Psalm 90:2 says, 'Before the mountains were brought forth, or ever thou hadst formed the earth and the world, even from everlasting to everlasting, thou art God.' God doesn't have to answer to us. This is where faith comes in. We know God is love. We know God is holy. But we don't know why He allows things like this. There are things we just can't understand in this life."

Tears welled up in the preacher's eyes as he spoke directly to the family. "Noah, Sara, family, thank God for the precious little girl He gave you. I know she was a joy to you as she was to many of us. God will not forsake you now. Psalm 91:4 says, 'He shall cover thee with his feathers, and under his wings shalt thou trust.' "

Once again a dark hole gaped in the sparkling snow of the graveyard. Surrounded by loved ones, the grieving family once more committed a body back to the dust. Songs about heaven evaporated in the frosty air.

Lunch afterward was a noisy affair with so many people crowded in the house. Sara ate quietly, keeping her thoughts to herself. *Life will have to go on.* Although she still felt battered, the love of the women around her comforted her. They, too, were mothers, and could empathize with the ache in her heart. *These are true friends,* she thought. *I know they will help me in the days ahead.*

Chapter

The dog cried.

Gloom settled over the Beachy household like a heavy blanket, muffling any enjoyment of life. The void loomed everywhere. The small rat terrier, who had considered Barbara Jean his best friend, moped about, scorning his food. The three older children, restlessly cooped up in the winter-bound house, were trying to understand and deal with the changes in their lives.

"Mommy, why did our babies have to die?" Judy cried after breakfast.

"I'm tired of everyone crying!" Mary Lou snapped.

Sara gathered her little girls and settled on the couch. Her work could wait. She wanted to savor the beauty of closeness with her living children. "Do you wonder what Barbara Jean and Henry might be doing in heaven right now?" she asked. "There's no way for us to really know, but I'm sure they're happy there with Jesus. Marvin, please bring the Bible storybook and let's look at the part that talks about heaven."

Marvin brought the well-worn *Egermeier's Bible Story Book*, and they all looked at the pictures. It did look wonderful, but they still missed their siblings!

"Children, we will be sad for a while, but remember that God is taking care of our babies. I want you to always love Jesus so when you get old and die, you can go to heaven too," Sara said. She hugged each one, and they went back to their play. Before long they were their lively selves again.

Unlike the children, Sara couldn't forget. Everywhere she saw reminders of their loss. The most painful time for her was when she put away the children's clothes. As she started the task one day, the lines of an old song ran through her thoughts, and she sang it softly . . .

> Mother, dear, come bathe my forehead,
> I am growing very weak;
> Let the clear and cooling water
> Fall upon my burning cheek.

Tell my loving little playmates
That I never more shall play;
Give them all my toys, but, Mother,
Put my little shoes away.

Now I'm growing tired, dear Mother,
Soon I'll say to you "good day;"
Always remember what I told you,
Put my little shoes away.

Mother, soon I'll be with Jesus,
'Ere perhaps another day;
Then, oh, then, my loving mother,
Put my little shoes away.[1]

Sara knew these clothes weren't special or fancy, but they had belonged to her cherished babies. Each piece had a memory connected with it. *Remember when Henry wore this the first time he went to church? Remember how Barbara Jean would wear this dress as she played quietly among the pretty flowers in the garden for hours? She had fit perfectly into that background! Remember when . . .* Sara pressed the worn garments to her face and cried unashamedly.

---

[1] Samuel Mitchell, public domain.

That night Sara had a beautiful dream. She saw a flower-lined pathway leading to heaven, and on it a happy, healthy Barbara Jean smiled and motioned to her mother as if to say, "Come here! Look what I found, Mama." The peacefulness and joy of that special dream calmed and comforted Sara for weeks.

* * * * * * * * * *

Striding to the table, Noah let the pile of mail fall with a thud. "Bills, bills, and more bills! I don't know how we are ever going to pay all these bills," he grumbled to Sara.

Sara's eyes begged him to be quiet. She didn't want the children to know how desperate they felt about finances. She shuffled through the pile. *Ferguson ambulance and embalming, $12.00. Columbus Children's Hospital, $41.20.* Sara didn't even want to open the rest.

"We can pay Ferguson, but the hospital will have to wait," Sara said. "We will just have to be more frugal."

"Do the best you can." Noah walked back out to the barn, his shoulders slumped with worry.

Lord, you know our needs, Sara prayed silently. *Thank you for the way the church and friends have been helping us. We have had so many gifts, but it is still hard. Please show me ways I can save money and be a helpmeet to Noah. Help me trust you and be content even as we scrimp to live.*

The days passed, filled with work. Hard work kept all of them from stagnating in their grief. To keep the family busy, Sara started her spring cleaning early. The children pitched in, relieved to find an outlet for their pent-up energy. Together they scrubbed the walls free of the grime that built up after heating with the woodstove all winter. They washed windows, wiped shades, and rearranged furniture.

Sara looked around her community with newly-enhanced sensitivity. *I wish I had my babies, but since I don't, I might as well help other people. There are needs I can meet. And it's good for Marvin, Mary Lou, and Judy to get out of the house. We all have so many sad memories here.*

No matter how busy she was, Sara often took time to write to her sisters.

March 9, 1946
Plain City
Dear Sisters,

Greetings in Jesus' holy name, who has died on the cross for us poor sinners. We are fine except for colds. Hope this finds you all in good health.

This is a foggy morning, but it isn't very cold. It sure has been warm and nice already the first part of this week.

Wilma, you know Mony Hershberger, the man that worked out here? They had a baby that weighed only 4½ pounds, but it was too weak to drink or suck. They fed it with a medicine dropper. Then it got choking spells. Last Sunday it got one (possibly while they weren't with it) and it had passed away when she picked it up to feed. They were away visiting at the time.

I had washed for them since their baby was born because they couldn't get a hired girl. I felt sorry for them. I washed and ironed. I didn't know what to charge, so I said $1.75 a week. I didn't feel that should be too much. I did their washing and cleaning Monday. I wanted to do that free of charge, when I think how much people have done for us! We went to Mony's place on

Monday and stayed there till Tuesday morning. We attended the funeral in the afternoon. The baby was 26 days old. The blessed little child! It was nice it could leave this sinful world.

On Sunday we went to church at Dan Helmuth's home.

Wednesday they had a sewing bee at Alvin Kramer's place.

We were gone very much the two weeks before this, helping people who needed to move. Six families moved from our church. We counted thirty children besides parents, so you can hardly imagine how much smaller the church is. These all moved to Iowa. I do hope they will like it since they have gone, but people felt sorry to see them go as we would have enjoyed having them here to help our church as well. But may God bless them.

We have 500 chicks. We got them Tuesday. They seem pretty hardy so far, although one was dead the other morning.

We saw Henry Yoder's family when they were

here. I talked a long time with his wife. In the eve we were over to Ira Yoder's place, then visited a while again. . . .

Say, Wilma, I would like to ask you a question. I wish you would answer on it as soon as you have decided whether you want to or not. Would you work for us beginning October 1 until in December or Christmas?

Sara smiled to herself as she wrote that question. Wilma had helped them last year when Henry was born, so she knew firsthand how lively the children were. Once Wilma and Sara had come in from chores to find Marvin, Mary Lou, and Judy gleefully spreading saltines on the floor and crushing them with the rocking chair. Maybe Wilma wouldn't be too excited about coming again!

. . . With God's help we expect a baby in the last part of October. If we wouldn't have liked you, we wouldn't have asked you back again. Ha! But suit yourself. Let me know so I have time to look around for someone else if you'd rather

not work for us. We were down to the hospital to see what we could find out about little Barbara a few weeks ago. We talked to the head man at the hospital. We got nice satisfaction.[2] *We sure miss the children a lot, although we know they're safe on that beautiful shore forevermore. If only we can meet them there some day.*

Best wishes,
Noah, Sara, & children

When you can, pray for us. We will do likewise, but in weakness.

P.S. We have received 85 sympathy cards and from 15 to 20 letters.

Deep in thought, Sara capped her pen. The outpouring of sympathy from so many people had amazed her. She thanked God for such loving friends. *But I'm so, so tired. Maybe after this new baby arrives I'll feel like my normal, cheerful self again. For now I can only hope.*

---

[2] Although the details of this conversation are unknown, it appears that the man explained to Noah and Sara the cause of Barbara Jean's death (pneumonia) and possibly apologized for the lapse in communication which caused them to not be notified immediately.

Chapter

Spring came!

I feel a spring in my step again, thought Sara with surprise. It seemed like a miracle! For months she had been doggedly putting one foot in front of the other, clinging to the Bible promises like "This poor man cried, and the LORD heard him, and saved him out of all his troubles" (Psalm 34:6), and "Call upon me in the day of trouble: I will deliver thee, and thou shalt glorify me" (Psalm 50:15). Now Sara found herself smiling, revitalized by the promise of new life both in the earth and in her womb.

"Children, Dad did the plowing this morning, so it's time to plant the garden!"

Eagerly the children grabbed light jackets and ran to

the shed for hoes. It was still too cold to go barefoot, but they didn't complain. They wanted to have those fresh, crisp vegetables as quickly as possible.

In a few weeks, peas, green beans, onions, and radishes pushed through the soil. Potatoes and strawberries, tomatoes and sweet corn; the sturdy seedlings promised abundance. Like many Amish housewives, Sara believed that no garden was complete without flowers. Zinnias, marigolds, and petunias bordered the vegetable plot, enclosing the well-tended rows with a show of color.

As spring turned to summer, Noah began spending long days in the field, leaving the chores to Sara and Marvin. Even the girls helped with feeding chicks and gathering eggs. On exceptionally nice days Sara packed a picnic lunch, and the whole family went out and met Noah in the field. Then they ate their lunch together in the shade of the fencerow.

• • • • • • • • • • •

"Everybody up!" Sara's voice bounced off the walls of the upstairs hallway. "We've got lots of beans to do today!"

"Mom, we're still tired," the girls groaned.

"I know, but it looks like it will be hot today, so let's get started."

Sara's example spurred the children to work hard. They picked the long rows of beans and then gathered in the shade to snap them before canning.

"Some jobs just aren't much fun," Sara told her children, "but did I ever tell you about the time..." Stories, laughter, and singing made the work go quickly.

• • • • • • • • • •

The fluffy yellow chicks quickly grew into chickens that had to be butchered. Sara appreciated her in-laws' help with that messy job. Together they packed the meat chunks into quart jars and canned them. Everyone was busy.

• • • • • • • • • •

"We need a break," Noah said to Melvin Kramer and Ab Miller one day. Close friends as well as neighbors, the three men often did things together. "We've all been working so hard, and there's no money to travel. Let's do something special that doesn't cost too much."

"I've got an idea," said Melvin. "I just bought that gypsy grocery wagon, you know, that I'm planning to turn into a spring wagon. Why don't we pack up the families and go down to the Columbus Zoo? There would be plenty of room for everyone, and I've heard the zoo is an interesting place."

"Super!" said Ab. "Let's make the trip this Saturday. It looks like the weather will be nice and warm."

Sara, Katie Kramer, and Mary Miller liked the idea immediately. *That's just what our children need*, Sara thought. *They haven't had nearly enough happy times this year.*

It was a jolly bunch that piled into the covered gypsy wagon on Saturday. They took the back roads to Columbus, enjoying the curious looks of passersby. Soon they had the horses tied up in a shady spot in the woods near the zoo, and the generous picnic lunch was spread. After lunch Noah fed the horses before the families headed over to the zoo.

"Let's go see the monkeys first." Judy pulled Noah's hand and danced in circles.

"I guess we could do that," Noah said, leading the way.

"Look at them swinging through the trees!" Mary Lou squealed.

"And that mom is scolding the baby over there," Judy giggled.

"Come on, girls," Marvin said. "Let's go see the lion."

Sara smiled as she watched their enthusiasm. How it refreshed her soul to see them happy and carefree, enjoying God's creation! *Thank you for this day, Lord,* she prayed silently.

Finally, reluctantly, the party turned homeward. Ab regaled them with lively harmonica music, but even so the children had fallen asleep by the time they got home. What a joyfully tiring day!

* * * * * * * * * *

By late July it was time for the wheat to be threshed. Wheat threshing always reminded Sara of the time early in their marriage when money had been especially tight.[1] How she had dreaded wheat threshing

---

[1] Noah was married at nineteen. As was common in Amish culture, Noah's father had expected him to still send part of his paycheck to his parents until he was twenty-one, so that contributed to the financial strain they felt during those years.

that year! They hadn't had the money to prepare the kind of meal the threshers expected. Those men could attack a meal like locusts, wiping it out. *What can I do?* she had fretted.

I'll fix goat meat, Sara had decided. Noah bought a nice goat for only two dollars. Sara smiled her approval when Noah had brought it home. *That meat will go a long way!*

On wheat threshing day, Sara and a neighbor lady had cooked up a feast of buttered vegetables, snowy mashed potatoes with gravy, homemade bread and jam, pudding made from their plentiful eggs and milk, and fresh apple pie. A savory goat-burger meatloaf stood on the center of the table as the main dish.

As the noisy, sweaty men tramped onto the porch and washed up at the big tin washtubs, Sara worried. She knew their neighbor Sam, one of the crew, had often boasted, "Nobody could feed me goat meat; I could smell it." She hoped the spices had done the trick.

After a silent prayer, the threshers had devoured the hearty meal. To Sara's relief, no one seemed to detect the goat meat. In fact, several commented on the delicious meatloaf as they took their second helping. Sara hid her amusement and decorously kept on serving.

After the meal, one of the men discovered what kind of meat they had been served. Laughing, he asked Noah, "What shall I do if the men start bleating this afternoon?" Of course, the men couldn't resist telling neighbor Sam about the goat meat he had eaten. It took a long time for him to live down that joke.

Sara smiled at the memory. *This year I hope we'll be able to afford more than goat meat.*

· · · · · · · · · ·

William was born at home on October 20, 1946. Mary Lou and Judy, ages five and four, fought for the privilege of holding the new baby brother. How they admired his blond hair, blue eyes, and Beachy pug nose! They thought it was about time they had another baby to play with.

"William, you are so special," Sara whispered. "I hardly have time to rock you at such a busy time of year, but you are more important than all the work around here." Joy bubbled up in Sara as she rocked. *I do wish it would have suited Wilma to be our maid again. Oh well, I will have to find a way to get things done myself. I'm just so happy to have a baby again!*

One Sunday afternoon the family piled into the buggy and went for a visit to Grandpa Beachy's. Noah's sister Florence and her husband Mark Hostetler had recently returned from Civilian Public Service in Warnersville, Pennsylvania. Like many other young Amish and Mennonites, Mark had served in stateside work crews when he was drafted during World War II because he conscientiously opposed going to war. Now, to welcome Mark and Florence back, several of the other brothers and sisters had gathered at the home place. They had a lively time of talking, joking, and eating popcorn.

Little William was passed around by the aunts and admired, but the attention didn't impress him. "He has had this cold all week." Sara patted the fretful baby's back. "I have tried everything I can think of, but he is still miserable."

Finally Noah said, "Let's just go home. There's not much point to visiting with such a fussy child."

William's cold grew steadily worse. Sara didn't become too worried until Thursday afternoon, when suddenly William seemed desperately sick. His temperature rose to 101 degrees, and his breathing became a dry, hacking cough. Frantically Noah and Sara called a driver, wrapped up William, and rushed him to the doctor. His cursory examination only increased their anxiety. "Take him to Children's Hospital right away."

"Oh, Noah, do you think they can help him?" asked Sara, dread and fear etched in her voice.

Noah shook his head. He could see a tinge of blue outlining William's lips, ears, and nose. Memories of the way Barbara Jean had died flooded his mind. "I don't know, but we don't have a choice." He shook his head again in resignation.

Repressed sobs blocked Sara's throat. Heartbroken but tearless, she clutched the blanketed child more tightly. All the way to Columbus she prayed silently. *Oh, God, I am so afraid for my baby. Please take care of him. Please don't let him die! Please!*

In her mind she recited Psalm 23 over and over. "*The LORD is my shepherd; I shall not want. . . . Yea, though I walk through the valley of the shadow of death, I shall fear no evil: for thou art with me . . .*" *Thou art with me. Thou art with me. Oh, God, please save my baby!*

Efficient but powerless, the hospital staff labored to save William's life. Already his little feet and hands had begun to grow cold. Everyone knew death was inevitable.

Hand in hand, Noah and Sara waited. "I don't understand why God is letting William die! I always thought God had good plans for His children," Sara cried in despair.

Noah's face was tight with grief and anger. "It isn't fair. We shouldn't have to go through this again."

"I'm so sorry." The doctor interrupted their conversation. "There is nothing more we can do. Would you like to hold him until he passes?"

Wordlessly Sara reached out her arms to cuddle tiny William. Tears dripped on his blanket as she rocked him back and forth. She wanted to hold him as long as she possibly could.

William died at 10:50 p.m., November 21, 1946. The doctor encouraged them to have an autopsy done, since this was the third family death in a year. The grim report read:

> *It appears that William had a sugar storage disease involving his heart, which caused it to become enlarged and to function poorly. While this is generally not compatible with life, it is not something which is commonly seen. There were no defects of the large vessels growing from the*

heart or abnormal openings in the heart itself. In addition to the heart disease, William had a chronic kidney disease of the right kidney which is not related to the above condition.

Since this kind of heart disease is quite rare and is generally not related to any family tendency, it is my feeling that it would be safe for you to have other children . . .

Sara questioned the doctor's conclusion. How could they be sure this condition would not affect future children? William's symptoms had been so much like Henry's. And William's heart had weighed fifty grams instead of the normal twenty-one. A heart that large made it difficult for a baby to breathe. Sara remembered how both Henry and Barbara Jean had struggled for each breath. The doctors told them there was no known cure for this heart disease. No hope was extended to the sorrowful couple as they left the hospital again with an invoice for $5.52 as their only keepsake.

How dismal the family felt as they prepared for yet another funeral! Sara moved in a shocked daze. *God, I always thought you were loving and kind. Why are you taking my beloved babies? It feels like I can't handle this grief, this hurting. I don't understand why! I want to trust you, but I'm overwhelmed with this sorrow. I'm so afraid that if we have more children, they'll have this problem too. I need your help! And Marvin, Mary Lou, and Judy are looking to us for security and comfort. I have nothing to give. I feel like an old, worn-out woman, and I'm just twenty-eight!*

Through her tears, Sara read Isaiah 40:30–31: "Even the youths shall faint and be weary, and the young men shall utterly fall: but they that wait upon the LORD shall renew their strength; they shall mount up with wings as eagles; they shall run, and not be weary; and they shall walk, and not faint." *Lord, only you can provide the strength I need.*

Church was held at Joe Beachy's that Sunday morning, so William's funeral took place there in the afternoon. Bleak, bare trees and gray skies completed the dreary scene. A tearful group surrounded another small grave in the quiet cemetery. This grave would not even be marked by a simple white stone like the graves of Henry and Barbara Jean. The family had no money for anything that was not absolutely necessary. Noah and Sara wept as they buried another baby.

Chapter

"Let's play funeral!"

The childish voices carried into Sara's kitchen. Puzzled, she watched the children frolicking in the fresh snow. They were putting Judy's doll into a shoebox and preparing to bury it in a shallow snow grave. Marvin, playing the role of the preacher, intoned a blessing over the grave.

Suddenly the emotions Sara had bottled up released themselves in passionate tears. She hurried to her bedroom and fell to her knees beside the bed. Uninhibited, she cried out, "Oh, God, what can I do? We've had so many deaths that my children act it out in their play! How can I make it through this sadness? There's nobody around to talk to. Nobody else has lost so many babies. I need your help, Lord!"

The Scripture she had read that morning in Psalm 91 came back to her. *"He shall cover thee with his feathers, and under his wings shalt thou trust: his truth shall be thy shield and buckler. Thou shalt not be afraid for the terror by night . . . For he shall give his angels charge over thee, to keep thee in all thy ways."* Eventually the tears subsided, and Sara felt the peace of God's sheltering wings again.

Sara thought back over the dream she had had recently. She had seen her three babies in heaven, holding glowing candles. As she watched them, Barbara Jean's candle went out. In her dream, Sara asked Barbara Jean why her candle didn't keep burning, and the child said, "Because you keep crying. Your bitter tears put it out."

The dream convicted Sara. *Am I still bitter about Barbara Jean's death?* she asked herself. *Yes, it was the most difficult one to go through, yet, deep down, I know God is trustworthy. No matter what I face, I must give up my will and accept God's will.*

"I will trust you," she prayed in renewed commitment. Sara opened her hands in surrender. "Lord, I give you my sorrow, my anger. All of my life is yours. But I need courage from you each day! Make me a faithful wife and mother. Help me teach these children about you. My work ahead is clear; I don't want to be so caught up with wishing my babies had lived that I fail to treasure each moment you give me with my living children."

Later Sara copied a poem by an unknown author and placed it between the leaves of her thick English-German Bible:

> Life is made of volumes three:
> The past, the present, and yet to be.
> The past is done and laid away;
> The present we live from day to day;
> But the last of these, volume three,
> Is hidden from sight, and God holds the key.

Thus resolved, Sara went on with daily life. Marvin had started school, and Mary Lou and Judy kept each other occupied. Yet in spite of Sara's desire to live in the present, she realized the babies' deaths had left an indelible imprint on their lives. As she thought back over the past year, she realized her children had become more susceptible to fear than they used to be.

Some of these scary moments happened at chore

time. As soon as they were old enough, Sara began leaving the three children in the house while she helped Noah with the milking. One evening Noah and Sara came back in to find all three of them cowering behind the couch.

"What's wrong?" Sara asked, concerned.

"There's somebody looking in the window," Mary Lou said.

Noah turned to Marvin for clarification.

"We were playing, and we heard a noise on the porch and then on the window. When we looked up, there was this face staring in at us! I think it was just the goat, but it looked like it would break in and maybe hurt somebody . . ." Marvin tried to explain the fear that had gripped them all.

Several weeks later Noah and Sara came in to find the three lying on the couch, quieted once more by fear. "What's wrong?" they asked.

Timidly, little Judy pointed toward the stairway. "The mouse is coming out," she whispered.

A small nose stuck out suspiciously under the door. When Noah walked over and opened the door, the mouse didn't run. It was already dead!

Marvin had teased the girls unmercifully after that

for being scared of a little dead mouse. They were too young to remind him that he had lain on the couch, as scared as the rest of them, until their parents came in.

Judy didn't used to be scared of mice, Sara remembered. During the summer months on the Sundays not scheduled for church, the Amish held Sunday school at the Plainview Christian School building. While there one day, Judy had come back from the outdoor restroom, her face glowing with excitement.

"Look what I found, Mommy," she whispered. "Baby horsies!"

Curiously Sara peeked into the folded handkerchief Judy had thrust onto her lap. Inside were nine hairless baby mice!

"Judy," she whispered, choking back laughter, "these are baby mice. They still need their mommy. Run back out and put them where you found them, okay?"

Reluctantly Judy had put them back.

• • • • • • • • • •

How do I get ready for Christmas this year? Sara longed to create some happy memories for her brood. *We can't afford to spend much on presents. And it's hard to celebrate when our grief feels so fresh.* Finally, a week before Christmas, Noah and Sara did their meager shopping. Twilight was falling as they arrived home just in time for chores. Noah hid their purchases in a nearby shed while Sara settled the children in the house. "I'll fix supper as soon as we're done choring," she told them. "You just stay in here and play nice."

Marvin could hardly wait until Sara closed the door behind her. "I know where Daddy put the Christmas presents!" he said proudly. "I saw him carry the bags out to the shed. Let's go look at them."

Mary Lou and Judy considered this novel idea. Those brown bags had been tempting them all the way home from town. "Mom and Dad are choring," said Marvin. "They'll never find out."

"Okay, let's go," they told Marvin.

Quickly Marvin got out the flashlight, and they all put on their coats. A quiet but excited trio followed the yellow beam to the shed.

"What is it? What is it?" Judy fairly danced with anticipation as the older two carefully pulled items out of the bags.

"Well, it looks like you get dolls this year, and I have a tractor," Marvin said, tucking the items back in the bags.

"We'd better get back inside before Mommy and Daddy catch us," said Mary Lou, glancing around guiltily.

They hurried back to the house.

From the barn Noah noticed the flickering flashlight trail and guessed immediately what had happened. *That Marvin,* he thought. *I'm going to have to teach him a lesson.*

Noah knew the truth of the saying, "Spare the rod, and spoil the child." Marvin learned a lesson that night—never use a flashlight if you want to fool Daddy about where you've been!

During these months, Sara discovered that the children explored their world eagerly, often testing the boundaries she and Noah had set. Marvin was not the only one who needed to learn what was acceptable behavior. The girls also learned about Daddy's knack for discovering misbehavior that winter.

"Have you ever tried going barefoot in the snow?" Mary Lou asked Judy one day.

"No."

"Well, I think it would be kinda fun. Let's just run around the house once and see what it's like!"

"Okay."

They found out it was very cold, and their punishment after Daddy saw their tracks convinced them not to try that again.

Another afternoon the girls were holding a tea party with their new dolls upstairs in the bedroom. "Okay, now we have to wash dishes," Judy announced. "I'll bring up some water from downstairs."

Mary Lou was surprised at this suggestion. "I don't think Mommy and Daddy would like that, but . . . I guess they'll never find out."

In the bustle of cleaning up their party, a movement at the end of the lane caught Mary Lou's attention. "Daddy's back! Hurry up and get rid of that water!"

In her haste Judy knocked the edge of the table and spilled some water. "How are we gonna clean it up?" she worried.

Resourceful Mary Lou grabbed a large handful of toilet paper, soaked up the water, and threw the sodden mess out the window onto the sloping roof of the porch below. "There, everything looks okay."

But Noah saw the paper on the roof and knew something was up. Another spanking for the girls was in order.

• • • • • • • • •

"Well, Mom, I have some news for you." Sara and her mother-in-law were husking sweet corn together in the summer of 1947. "We're expecting another baby."

"So how are you feeling?" Mary Ann asked.

"I'm a bit worried," Sara said. "Don't tell anyone else yet. I'm going to hide it as long as I can. I just hope everything will be okay. On one hand I'm excited. Judy is already five, and I do love babies. On the other hand, I don't want to get my heart set on it. Who knows if the baby will be healthy?"

Sara pushed aside the nagging worry by staying busy helping others around her. Noah's sister Betty was married in December, and his brother Alvin was planning to marry in February, so she spent several days helping her mother-in-law.

Verda arrived on Sunday, January 24, 1948. What delight the new baby brought to the whole family, especially her two big sisters! They loved to hold her and play with her. Marvin, disappointed at first that the baby wasn't a boy, soon adored her as much as the other children did. Automatically the household centered itself around this precious little one.

At six weeks of age Verda developed a bad cold. Instantly the family plunged into despair. The symptoms were all too familiar. Henry . . . Barbara Jean . . . William . . . all of them had started out with "colds" only days before their deaths. Despite the doctor's assurance that this heart disease wasn't a genetic tendency, they feared it was only a matter of time until Verda, too, was dead.

The doctor's orders to take her to Children's Hospital confirmed the family's fears. Yet they had no alternative. Resigned, Noah and Sara took Verda down to Columbus. She was admitted immediately with a diagnosis of broncho-pneumonia.

This time Sara had her heart set on staying overnight, and their new doctor, Dr. Herman Karrer, encouraged her to do that.

"Sara, are you sure you are okay here by yourself? What if Verda dies?" Noah asked as he reluctantly picked up his coat.

"I will be fine. I know things don't look good, but I am not going through what we did with Barbara Jean. Go on home. The driver is waiting, and the children need you." Sara gently pushed him toward the door.

* * * * * * * * *

It was a long night for Sara. She sat next to the oxygen-tented little girl, holding the dimpled hand. Memories of her other babies paraded through her tired mind. As she prayed and crooned soft nothings to the baby, Sara began to notice a difference in the infant's condition. *She doesn't seem to be getting worse.* As the first rays of morning light filtered into the hospital room window, joy dawned in Sara's heart. *She actually seems to be improving!* The baby's breathing was relaxed, her pulse steady, and her cheeks showed a flush of pink color.

The nurse confirmed Sara's intuitive diagnosis. "It looks like a few days in here should get her back as good as new," she told Sara.

Sudden hope flooded Sara's entire being. "Lord, thank you! Thank you!" she whispered as she hurried to call home with the good news. "Verda is getting better! She's going to make it!"

In the yard around the old farmhouse, the buds on the shade trees began to swell, fat with the promise of spring. And what a happy spring it was! Sara almost enjoyed paying the hundred-dollar hospital bill. Her baby was well worth it! Verda delighted the family with her antics and accomplishments. At six months she could stand fearlessly in one of Noah's big hands while he raised her to the ceiling. He had also taught the older children to perform that feat, but Verda was especially adept at it.

One summer evening Noah and Sara were relaxing on the porch while the children played tag in the yard. Verda bounced on Sara's lap. Smiling at her young brood, Sara told Noah, "Our children are such a gift. Let's hold them near while we have them."

Noah didn't answer for a long moment. Yet by now their mutual understanding had deepened; even his silence spoke volumes to Sara. She knew the void he felt in his heart when he thought of the children they could no longer hold. She felt it too.

"Yes," he said quietly. "Let's."

Chapter

Rain drummed the roof.

"Sara, it's time to get up." Noah prodded his wife.

"Oh, Noah, I don't feel good. Can you start chores and let me sleep a little longer? Then come back and wake me up."

"Well, all right." His tone sounded reluctant. Sara heard his heavy tread as he left the room. Then he paused and returned.

"I think I'll call Eli Yutzys[1] and ask if I could bring the girls down there for the morning. Then you can

---

[1] The reader may notice that the Amish often use a phrase such as "Eli Yutzys" or "Marvins" when referring to a couple or to a family. These and other Pennsylvania Dutch expressions have been retained in the dialogues to reflect the culture of the family.

rest better," he told her.

"Okay, thanks. Be sure to put a scarf on Verda. She's starting with another cold."

Gratefully Sara stretched out again. She hadn't been feeling well with this latest pregnancy in the summer of 1948. *It feels so good to stay in bed!* she thought. Through the fog of her weariness, she heard Noah wake the girls.

A nagging anxiety dogged Noah's steps. He went about his chores mechanically. Sara so seldom complained about aches and pains that he feared something was really wrong. Finally he went back in the house to check on her.

"Noah, you'd better call the doctor. This seems serious," Sara told him. Her voice sounded painfully weak. She didn't tell him she could almost feel blood draining from her arms. "Oh, God, please protect our unborn child," she whispered.

Noah rushed to the phone and dialed Dr. Karrer. "I'm sorry; he's not here right now, but I'll try to reach him," Margaret Karrer said. "We'll be over as soon as we can."

"I'll call Dr. Ingmire." Noah decided. "I don't think he's as good a doctor, but we need help."

The minutes stretched like hours until Dr. Ingmire

drove in. Noah piled nine blankets on Sara in a vain attempt to warm her up. Her face grew paler all the time.

The doctor walked into the bedroom to examine the patient. After a cursory check, he said, "I'm sorry, I don't think there is anything we can do."

Noah stared at him in disbelief. "You've got to help, Doctor! Can't we take her to the hospital? You must do something!" Despair gripped him.

Just then Dr. Karrer and his nurse wife Margaret came rushing in, toting their equipment. A quick examination showed them the gravity of the situation. They sprang into action.

"Call the ambulances—both of them," Dr. Karrer ordered. "Whoever gets here first will take her in. Margaret, the saline solution."

His order was unnecessary. Margaret had seen many transfusions during World War II, and she already had the precious glass bottle in hand. She had only one, but one would suffice. Quickly she set up the IV, clamping it to the high, white-painted metal headboard. She had the needle in place, the bottle ready to connect.

Clang! In her haste the bottle hit against the metal. The nurse caught her breath. If that bottle was broken, Sara would die. But it wasn't! Her forehead creased with concern, Margaret set up the saline solution, hoping against hope that they weren't already too late. She breathed a sigh of relief as she watched the essential fluid drip through the tube into the depleted veins.

Noah stepped out of the room for a few moments to call their neighbor Melvin Kramer. Melvin scribbled a note to his wife and immediately came over to Noah's house. He took in the situation at a glance. "Marvin and I will take care of the rest of the chores. You don't have to worry about a thing at home," he told Noah.

The Ferguson ambulance won the race up the long lane and backed up to the door. In a matter of seconds, the ambulance crew had loaded the now-unconscious woman. Out the driveway they flew!

The driver, Charles Jay Ferguson, looked back to check on his patient. Dr. Karrer just gestured commandingly—DRIVE!

Sirens wailed. From the neighbor's living room Judy heard the sound, and it struck terror in her heart. Tears rolled down her cheeks. Lizzie Yutzy tried to console her, but Judy refused to be comforted. She sat in a small rocker looking at a Bible storybook picture of angels.

"Judy, God's taking care of your mommy."

"No," Judy sobbed, shaking her head. "Mommy's

going to be an angel." She sniffed pitifully.

"Oh, Judy," Lizzie knelt beside the six-year-old and hugged her tightly. "Let's pray for her."

Silent and grim-faced, Noah sat beside his wife, holding her cold, white hand. They had shared a lot of sorrow, but it had been *together*. If he lost her, how could he handle it? "Would that driver speed up?" he muttered. A glance at the speedometer showed they were already going ninety miles per hour. The hum of the tires became a prayer. "Let her live, let her live. Your will be done, but please let her live."

Meanwhile Dr. Karrer fought for Sara's life. At the edge of Columbus, they met the police escort Margaret had summoned. They needed all the help they could get!

The ambulance screeched in at the closest hospital in Columbus, the White Cross. They wheeled Sara straight through the operating doors, but the attending doctors shoved the stretcher back out. "This woman is dead."

"She is *not* dead!" Dr. Karrer pushed her back in authoritatively. "Get busy!"

· · · · · · · · ·

"Noah, I think she'll live." Dr. Karrer's face looked haggard, yet relieved, as he talked to Noah several hours later. "It was a tubal pregnancy that ruptured. She lost about seven pints of blood, some of which we were able to transfuse back into her body during surgery. It will take a long time to recover her strength, but she'll live."

"Thank the Lord!"

How the family rejoiced when Sara came home from the hospital several weeks later! The near-tragedy reminded Noah and the children how much they needed and valued Sara. Neighbors had provided delicious food and regular transportation to the hospital. Aunt Christena and others had taken care of baby Verda. Sara's family had butchered a beef for them. Their physical needs had been met, yet there was no one like their mother to give encouragement and keep things running smoothly. Even the disappointment of missing the trip to Indiana for Aunt Wilma's August wedding paled in the face of what could easily have been. Thank God, Mommy was alive and home again!

Chapter

"Andy-over!"

Twilight calls of children at play provided a pleasant background for the adults' chatter. The families of Al Helmuth, Melvin Kramer, Ab Miller, and Noah Beachy spent many evenings together, often playing table games or throwing horseshoes. Tonight the men had played with the children awhile, but now they were cranking the well-worn ice cream maker on the porch.

"This ice cream just won't freeze tonight." Al rubbed his tired arm. Just then his wife Amanda called from the door, "Hey, if you men want some ice cream, we need the canister to put the mix in!"

Sheepishly the men gave her the cold, well-cranked canister. "All that work for nothing!"

The men's conversation turned to their latest cooperative venture, trash hauling. "In fact, I just found out about this auction coming up on Thursday." Ab pulled a sale bill from his pocket.

"It looks like they have a lot of old metal parts for sale." Melvin scanned the paper in Ab's hand.

"I think we should go," Noah said. "As long as they are paying a good price in Columbus for scrap, it is worth our time."

"I'll get the truck ready then." Ab smiled. "I'm hungry for some of those White Castle burgers on the way back."

"Nothing like seven-cent burgers and a glass of ice-cold pop." Noah nodded, rubbing his stomach.

The women, meanwhile, were busy talking as they worked on their embroidery and other handwork projects. "Rachel Miller said she will work for us this fall when the baby is born," Sara said. "I've heard she's a good worker."

"Yes, she is, but if you need any more help, just let us know!" Amanda said.

• • • • • • • • •

Sara had made all the needed preparations by September 16, 1949, when baby Howard arrived. Noah called the doctor out to the house, and Rachel came to assist in any way she could. Guarded joy surrounded the arrival of this child. As Judy, age seven, sadly put it, "When we have a baby, I just expect another funeral."

Sara didn't let the uncertainty keep her spirits down. She often told the children, "I know you have plenty of work to do, but why don't you just drop everything and come listen to this Bible story while I iron?"

"Mom, we know all these Bible stories about Daniel and the lions and David and Goliath. Tell us something new," Mary Lou begged.

Sara thought a moment. *What could I say to help my children understand the depth of God's love? They have been through so much loss already in their short lives. How can I encourage them?*

"Well, I can tell you something God did just for me."

"What was it?" Judy looked up eagerly.

"One day I was walking out behind the house, and I heard my name."

"And . . . ?" Marvin was not impressed.

"There was no one around, but I heard it as plain as day, 'SARA!' "

"Who was it?" Mary Lou asked.

"It was God! God called my name. Isn't it amazing how God cares about each of us individually? We have had hard times, but we also need to count our blessings. Can you think of any blessings?"

"Well, we have a new baby." Judy smiled.

"Yes, we do, and isn't he sweet?"

"Last summer you almost died, but God saved your life," Mary Lou said soberly.

"That's right," Sara said. "Now, run and play. I think Howard is hungry again."

* * * * * * * * *

Sara passed her tranquility of spirit on to others. Rachel, their maid, was struggling with teenage problems and had many questions about Scripture and joining the Amish church. While doing the housework, she found it easy to talk to Sara about the things that troubled her. "Sara, how do you know for sure if you are going to heaven? If I join the church, will that save me?"

"Oh, Rachel, I remember how worried I was at your age! The only way to be saved is to trust in Jesus. You know that the reason Jesus was crucified was to pay the penalty for our sins, right?"

"Yes, but surely I have to live right too, don't I?" Rachel asked. "I do so many wrong things!"

"Nobody can live perfectly enough to go to heaven! Living by rules doesn't save you. You need to ask Jesus into your heart by confessing your sins and asking Him to forgive you. That is salvation."

"I've done that, so why do I need to be baptized at all?"

"Baptism is an outward symbol of what happened inside you. After you are saved, then you obey the Bible because you love Jesus and want to please Him. We can't do this in our own strength. The same power that raised Jesus from the dead now lives in our hearts and helps us to do what is right. Does that make sense?"

"Well, yes. I do want to do what is right. Pray for me that I will have peace."

"Of course I will. And, Rachel, keep reading your Bible, especially the book of 1 John. That will help you know that Jesus has forgiven you and that you are a Christian."

"I will. Thanks, Sara!"

· · · · · · · · ·

Sara's dad, Henry Hochstetler, died only four days after Howard's birth. Sara had deeply appreciated her dad and the practical support he had offered her in the last several years. Not only had her parents made many trips to Ohio to comfort them in times of crisis, but they had also helped in more tangible ways, like butchering a beef for them. Much as she longed to be with her family during this time of grief, her first priority was her new baby.

"I hate to miss the funeral," she told Noah, "but I don't feel well enough to travel to Indiana so soon after giving birth."

"Well, you know how you feel. Maybe it would be better if you stayed home, and Marvin and I go."

When they returned, Marvin expressed his disappointment over the trip. "No, I didn't have a good trip. It was awful cold for September, and everyone was crying. The cousins didn't have much time for fun or playing together. I hate funerals! A funeral for a grownup is even worse than one for a baby! And I'm going to miss Dawdy so much!"

There was no shortage of work to do in the Beachy household. By now Mary Lou and Judy were old enough to help with simple tasks, but dawdling seemed more to their liking. Rachel found it necessary to punish them at times for their pokiness, but they still considered her a kind and loving *maud* (maid).

Several weeks later Rachel was helping with the chores when Sara came out with a phone message for her. "You'd better go to the hospital right away," she said. "Your dad's been hurt in a farm accident, and they want you to come."

So Sara again took on the full workload of household duties since Rachel needed to stay home and care for her father. Once again Sara's normal efficiency reasserted itself. She knew how to make the dust and dishes fly, and she often did so with a song.

As baby Howard grew, so did the family's attachment to him. Still, the occasional bluish tinge around his mouth and fingernails warned that all was not well. In late October Noah and Sara finally took him to Children's Hospital for an X-ray to see if his heart was enlarged like William's had been.

The next night Sara was trying to get back to sleep after Howard's restless, sickly cry finally quieted in slumber. Troubled thoughts tumbled about in her mind. *I'm so afraid Howard is going to die. Father God, please be merciful! He is your child, but we love him so much.* Sara tossed and turned. She sighed. *I need to get some sleep. It will be morning before I'm ready.* She closed her eyes resolutely, but suddenly she jerked awake. Something had changed. A mysterious light illuminated the room! Looking fearfully toward the cradle, Sara saw the softly glowing wings of an angel hovering over the sleeping child, and then the angel disappeared silently through a window. She blinked her eyes for a better look. "The angel is gone," she whispered. A tremor passed over her. "And so is my baby." Grief mixed with awe washed over her as she rose to check on Howard.

It was November 1, 1949. Somehow the vision of the angel eased Sara's sorrow, reminding her that her little one had gone to be with God. She felt new strength to offer the rest of her grieving family as another small, unmarked grave joined the row in the cemetery.

Sara held fast to the comfort of her angel vision. Although she shared it with the family, she cautioned the children not to tell anyone else. *People won't understand,* she thought. *They'll think I'm either bragging or going crazy with grief. But I know that's not the case. In His love, God reached down to send me a special message. I am loved! God does care about me and my suffering family. He provides for me a "secret place" just like Psalm 91:1 says. No matter what trials I face, I will choose to abide in the shadow of the Almighty and keep putting my trust in Him.*

Chapter 4

A quiet year passed.

> *March 16, 1951*
> *Dear Sister,*
>
> *Greetings in Jesus' holy name. We are all fine except Verda does not seem to feel so good since we are at home.*[1]
>
> *Our 350 chicks are supposed to come this morning. We aren't raising too many broilers—just pullets.*

---

[1] They had just returned from a trip to Indiana the previous weekend.

We came home about 7:30. We had to wait 3½ hours in Lima. We could have had it nice if we would have taken the 9:20 bus.

It was raining all the way to Lima, and from there it was snowing. It's snowing this morning again.

The fires were out when we came home. Of course, it was not unexpected for us since the choreboy isn't too old and neither is Marvin. They had a good time anyway.

Best wishes. I want to write to Mother also.

Noah, Sara, and family

Sara sighed to herself as she finished the short letter. The fire hadn't been the only thing Marvin neglected. Her yellow pet canary had starved to death as well. Marvin had been so sorry and apologetic. *I guess he'll grow up soon,* she reminded herself.

"Sara, I have an idea," Noah said one day.

"What's that?"

"Well, no matter how hard we work, we just are not making enough money here on this farm. I was talking to Ab today, and they like it over in Resaca. What would you think of moving down there?"

Sara pictured the area southwest of Plain City. It would be a long buggy ride from some of her friends, but if the move helped them pay their bills, she would be willing. At least Ab's wife Mary would be close by again. And people said the land over there was much more productive. "Are there any farms available to rent?"

"Ab said the Pearl Price farm is available. The house is pretty old, but the rent is reasonable." So they decided to move to the big, rambling, old farmhouse with rough, wooden floors. Sara scrubbed and painted.

"It's beginning to look like home." Noah surveyed her work.

"Yes, it does. Maybe the worst of our troubles are past." Sara picked up her paintbrush again.

"I sure hope so!"

The baby girl born in their new home on November 19, 1951, made it seem like a fresh, new beginning.

"What shall we name this baby?" Noah asked the older children.

Delighted with the prospect of picking a name, Mary Lou and Judy considered various possibilities. Finally they settled on "Miriam." Their Uncle John's wife was named Miriam, and she was much admired by the girls. Besides, the girls thought the name sounded elegant.

"Miriam it is," decided Noah and Sara. How they delighted in this dark-haired baby! Her round face was perfectly formed, and a dark curl hung over her forehead.

Many of their friends came over to see the new baby. Sara's nephew Omer Slabaugh and his wife Marie came to visit one day, carrying their young son Ernie all bundled up because of the cold. As they were unwrapping the cocoon of blankets, they suddenly exploded with laughter. They had been carrying poor little Ernie upside down! Sara joined in the laughter. This irrepressible nephew of hers had a cheerful attitude that was positively contagious. Yes, family and friends topped her list of blessings this Thanksgiving season.

The bubble burst on December 13. "Mommy, look at Miriam! Whenever she cries, her face turns blue," Mary Lou said.

Sara's heart sank. *That can mean only one thing. Miriam is going to die.* She called Dr. Karrer immediately. The following day Miriam was admitted into Children's Hospital.

"Her cyanosis is quite pronounced," the doctor

told the worried parents. "She is in cardiac failure." However, with Digitoxin (a medication to strengthen her heart), oxygen, and lots of fluids, she seemed to improve. During her stay, doctors took a small sample of muscle tissue. They wanted to see if Miriam showed any signs of the glycogen storage disease they suspected as the cause of the other deaths. They did find some glycogen present in the muscle, but at that time they were unable to determine if it was an abnormal amount.

Just in time for Christmas, Miriam came home to be with her family. Mary Lou and Judy spent a lot of time rocking their baby sister. They faithfully wore face masks to protect Miriam from germs. Grandma Hochstetler came from Indiana for an extended visit.

"Oh, Mom, I am so glad for your help!" Sara exclaimed. "Do you mind caring for Miriam so Verda and I can go to the school program this afternoon?"

"Of course not!" Mary loved her grandchildren, and she wanted to help Sara all she could.

After New Year's Day, Sara wrote to Barbara on a penny postcard:

Dear Sister,
Greetings in Jesus' holy name. I'm ashamed I

didn't answer your welcome letter. I don't know how to thank you enough for the box of things. You have done so much already! It made me feel kind of guilty to use all the nice things. We have snow, and it is pretty cold.

We took the baby to the hospital last night. The doctor gave her very little hope. She has the heart ailment. They're doing what they can. She is blue and very weak since her last shot. I'm trying to get ahold of Noah. He left at 7:00 a.m.

I'll end with love to all. Miriam is sleeping. I hope she sleeps right on and need not suffer more on earth if she can't get well.

Pray for us,
Noah, Sara, and family

P. S. Miriam seems a little better this afternoon.

On January 8, Sara was up all night. Miriam could take only a bit of milk, and in the morning their neighbor, Ed Miller, took them to the hospital. Miriam was in obvious distress. Her pitiful crying made the trip to Children's Hospital seem like an eternity.

The hospital staff could do nothing. By the time Ed got home, Noah had called again. "Could you come down and get us again? The baby just died."

Sara wept as she recorded her feelings in the privacy of her diary:

> *January 9, 1952, Wednesday: Took Miriam to the hospital. She had great pain, cried hard, and died at 9:00. Sad was the hour, but safe is her soul. Came home about 2:00. Soon many people came.*
>
> *January 10, 1952, Thursday: Many people were here and showed respectful sympathy. We find ourselves very small and feel like we have done little for people compared to what they have done for us.*
>
> *January 11, 1952, Friday: Today was sweet little Miriam's funeral. Two carloads came from Indiana. Had funeral at Joe Detweiler's place. Buried in new cemetery with the other four children.*

For Sara's three-year-old niece, Edna Mae Troyer,

these baby funerals were a new experience. "Why is there such a big hole for such a small box?" she asked innocently.

Sara echoed a similar question in her heart. *How can such a little girl leave such a big hole in my life?*

Chapter 4

Noah's still in bed.

Sara sipped her tea thoughtfully as she wrote the entry in her diary. This was becoming repetitious and worrisome. Noah had been sick off and on all spring and summer. He was losing weight, and he had spells of severe pain. In spite of taking X-rays and blood tests, the doctors didn't exactly know what was wrong. They said he had colitis, but no treatments seemed to be effective.

I think I know why he's ailing. Sara closed her diary and fastened the clasp. *I think he's just reacting to all the stress he's been under. He is such a private person. We've lost five children in the last six years, and he's bottled up all that pain. And I think he's ashamed of the fact that we can't get ahead financially. He compares himself with his dad and brothers and feels inferior.*

"Oh, God," she murmured. "Please heal Noah. You are the only One who can solve his problems."

The financial squeeze they had felt earlier had become even more oppressive. Miriam's $244.58 hospital bill was staggering. They could barely scrape the money together to meet the $15.00 monthly payment. Now Noah needed frequent medical treatments too. Sara tried to be as frugal as possible. They grew a big garden, and Noah fished and hunted as often as he could. When Sara felt burdened, she often turned to Philippians 4:11 and 13: "Not that I speak in respect of want: for I have learned, in whatsoever state I am, therewith to be content. . . . I can do all things through Christ which strengtheneth me."

Oh, why, then, do I find it so hard to be content? Sara wondered. On one of their trips to Indiana, Sara confided in her sister Wilma. "I have to be so careful when I buy groceries. Our children get hungry for things and beg just like other people's children, but I can't afford Kool-Aid and things like that. I can't even buy fresh fruits and vegetables to help my children stay healthy. It's so frustrating!"

Even harder was learning to accept all the help they were given, in spite of the good intentions of the givers. Yet without the aid of the community, Noah and Sara would never have made it. Neighbors came and helped plow, plant, and chore. Sara's sister Christena bought linoleum for the kitchen and helped put it in. Later Sara found a poem by an unknown author that helped her keep a proper perspective about money:

> Money will buy a bed, but not sleep.
> Money will buy books, but not brains.
> Money will buy food, but not appetite.
> Money will buy a house, but not a home.
> Money will buy medicine, but not health.
> Money will buy amusement, but not happiness.
> Money will buy a church, but not heaven.

Some people helped by just being friends. One evening Omer Slabaugh brought his family over. He had everyone laughing until 2:00 in the morning with the humorous stories he could tell.

But in spite of distractions like friendly storytelling, Noah was still sick. One neighbor didn't think Noah would live much longer, so he talked to Noah's landlord about renting the farm.

You don't know the Beachys, Sara thought when she heard that. *They don't give up.* And Sara didn't give up either. She raised chickens, did butchering, kept the house in order, and even helped relatives when she could.

It was Sara who took care of all the details. The family often laughed about the time when she had noticed Marvin's dirty ears one morning on the way to church. "Marvin Ray, didn't you wash your ears this morning?" A frown creased Sara's forehead. "You can't go to church like that! We're going past Eli Hochstetler's place. Run in and ask them for a wet soapy washcloth. Maybe that will help you remember next time!"

It was also Sara's duty to encourage the children in their work at Plainview Christian School. None of them liked school, and they often found the work difficult. Sara frequently had to scold her oldest son. "Marvin, I know you enjoy drawing cars, but you're going to have to spend more time on your lessons!"

The polio epidemic that swept through the country that year of 1952 hit Plain City hard, leaving numerous children and a few adults hospitalized, some paralyzed for life. For weeks the Amish didn't have church or school to avoid spreading the dreaded disease. Even when services resumed, children were not allowed to attend at first. Thankfully, polio didn't hit the Beachy children. *The Lord knows how much we can handle!* Sara reminded herself.

Although the older children had many responsibilities, they found time for fun as well. Marvin discovered the challenge of motors and rigged up a motorized bicycle on which his cousin John Henry lost two front teeth.

The children made friends with Paul Christner, who sometimes stayed with them when Noah and Sara traveled. Paul always seemed to have spending money, which made him an instant hero with the Beachy bunch.

"Let's go to the general store and buy some candy," he suggested to Marvin one day.

"Sure, let's go," Marvin agreed.

Off they went on horseback. Gleefully they bought as much candy as they could stuff in their pockets and took off for home to enjoy it.

"Wait a minute! Where did all the candy go?" Marvin asked, dismayed at finding his pockets almost empty when they reached the house.

"Hey, mine's gone too!" Paul turned his pockets inside out. "It must have fallen out during that wild ride!"

Upon retracing their route, the boys found their candy scattered on the ground. The squashed treats still tasted delicious!

* * * * * * * * *

So much has changed this year, Sara thought one evening as she packed boxes for yet another move. *Our old barn burned down, and Melvin and Katie Kramer's baby died in July. Noah's youngest brother Eli and his family moved to Cleveland. Crist and my sister Christena have gone to Florida for the winter. Noah had so many doctor visits and treatments, but he is finally feeling better! Now with this move to his folks' old home place, we'll be on a good farm with a modern milking set-up. Noah's dad even has a system for growing fresh oat sprouts year-round for the cattle. We can be a real help to his folks there, and maybe things will start going better for us again.*

Sara couldn't let her latest pregnancy slow her pace. December 4 was moving day, and they got settled into the small house next to Noah's parents' house. Since there was a lot of cornhusking left to do at the old Pearl Price place, Sara helped.

"Noah, I think the time has come to go to the hospital," Sara said after a full day of husking corn.

Noah didn't waste any time. Because of their previous problems, they had decided this child would be born in a hospital. Noah called a driver, and they arrived at the Marysville Hospital just twenty minutes before Wilma Irene was born on December 15, 1952.

Once again the Beachy family felt a cautious optimism. For the moment they were blissfully ignorant of the depressing family history note Dr. Karrer had filed in his medical report for the Marysville Hospital: *"Five of these apparently normal children have died between the ages of 6 wks. and two years, within a few hours of having contracted a mild upper respiratory ailment. [Three] . . . died in acute cardiac failure at Children's Hospital. Autopsy findings revealed only a glycogen defect in heart muscles."*

By the time Christmas shopping and programs and family get-togethers were over, Sara desperately needed rest. But on January 3, Wilma got sick and was admitted to Children's Hospital. Sara stayed with her there through the oxygen, EKGs, medication, and X-rays.

When they left for home on January 8, Sara felt sure little Wilma wasn't hers to keep. "We'll love you while you're here," she whispered to the reddish-brown-haired bundle in her arms.

Sara tried to shield the rest of the children from her inner conviction that Wilma would not live. She found refuge again in the Psalms. She loved Psalm 71:6: "By thee have I been holden up from the womb; thou art he that took me out of my mother's bowels: my praise shall be continually of thee." *Wilma's life is in God's hands. I must submit to His will. He is still worthy of my praise.*

Sara fondly stroked the black cover of her thick English-German Bible. Electrical tape held the binding together by now, and she often left it open beside the rocking chair. How she needed the strength God provided through His Word! Day by day He enabled her to keep the household functioning and her other children happy even when her heart was breaking. But one day Marvin saw tears rolling down Sara's cheeks as she rocked the baby.

"Is the baby sick, Mom?" he asked.

Sara tried to brush away her tears and quiet his worry, but she knew he understood.

Meanwhile Noah's parents had left for a winter in

Florida. While they were away, Noah and Sara could live in the bigger farm house instead of the little house. Sara, her niece Verna (the *maud* for this baby), and the girls ambitiously cleaned the big house and moved the family belongings over for several months. How good it felt to have room to stretch!

Although Wilma kept growing and developing almost normally, Sara never felt at ease. Finally, on Friday, January 23, Noah and Sara took Wilma to Children's Hospital again. She had been short of breath since the afternoon before, and that familiar blue shade was creeping over her face.

What a dreary, rainy winter day! Sara's thoughts kept returning to the Ben B. Miller family, whose child Edwin had died from a blood clot. *That funeral is today. I know just what they're going through.*

Holding back her tears, Sara waited as Wilma underwent more tests and treatments. She didn't need a medical expert to tell her that a pulse of 200 and a breathing rate of 112 respirations per minute was a serious condition. The X-rays showed Wilma's heart was enlarged even more than it had been previously. Doctors gave her morphine and oxygen and tried to get her to drink some juice with little success.

The day dragged on. Finally, close to 10:00 p.m., Noah and Sara left Room 450 for a short break. While they were gone, Wilma stopped breathing. Nurse Harris rushed to the station. "We need artificial respiration, NOW!" she ordered.

Dr. Beridge stepped in quickly, but in vain. "I'm sorry. She has expired," he told the couple when they returned.

"No!" The finality of death stunned Sara. Tearfully she reached out to touch her baby one more time.

Once again Noah signed an autopsy permit. Their five-week-old baby had a heart three times normal size as well as an enlarged spleen. Grimly they turned the body over to Paul Ferguson.

Another funeral. Sara cried all the way home. "I hope people don't pray that we have more children," she sobbed. "It hurts too much. We love them, take care of them, and then they're gone. Is it fair? We have to trust God. I know we have to trust God, but why are all these things happening to us?"

Sara closed her eyes in silent prayer. *Oh, Lord, I don't have enough strength! Help me through this sad hour. Thank you that dear little Wilma is now healthy with you, but comfort us now, I pray.*

Numbness settled over Sara like a cloak as she went through the appropriate motions. Soon relatives and friends flocked in. Late Sunday evening Noah's parents and Crist and Christena returned from Florida. Ab Miller's wife Mary made a beautiful white burial dress for Wilma.

The young folks came and sang. "Oh, come, angel band; Come and around me stand . . ."

Sara's sore heart drank in the comforting words. "Oh, bear me away on your snowy wings to my immortal home." Wilma had reached that safe and happy home already. *Thank God only her body is in that casket!* Sara thought.

The funeral was held at the old home place. Finally Noah's family lived in a place large enough to hold the funeral. Sim Yoder, Eli Nissley, and Noah Troyer preached the sermons. A freezing wind seemed to drive the hurt even deeper into the hearts of the aching Beachy family. One more hope was lost.

The *Plain City Advocate* carried a bleak front-page obituary on January 28, 1953:

INFANT DAUGHTER DIES IN HOSPITAL

Wilma Irene Beachy, age 1 month and 8 days,

infant daughter of Mr. and Mrs. Noah Beachy of Canaan Township died in Children's Hospital in Columbus, Friday, January 23. Services were held at the home Monday afternoon, burial in the Amish Cemetery.

Sara wept as she clipped out the newspaper article. *It doesn't look like major news to the rest of the world,* she thought, *just another baby that died. But Wilma was my baby. Oh, Lord, I loved her so much!*

Chapter

"I'm so tired!"

The gauntlet of grief had left Sara exhausted. As family members left for their faraway homes on Tuesday, she grew more and more weary. On Wednesday she allowed herself one day of rest and retrospection. *Life must go on,* she told herself the next day. Pushing her fatigue into the background, she processed her grief by venting her frustration on any dirt in sight. Since Sara's mother, Mary, had stayed in Ohio for a month to help out, they tackled the project together. They cleaned the house from top to bottom again, washing bedding, waxing floors. They raked the lawn and even cleaned the brooder house.

"We've been working so hard, Mom. I think we

should go visiting for a day," Sara said one morning after the three oldest children left for school. "Verna can keep Verda here, and we can go visit."

Mary readily agreed, and they were off. They stopped at Pin Kauffman's place and Henry Yoder's, then ended the day by visiting Sara's nephew Omer Slabaugh and his wife Marie. Since Omer's family had lived next to Henry and Mary's house for a number of years, Mary especially enjoyed that visit.

"How are you doing, Sara?" Marie asked.

Tears welled in Sara's eyes. "It is so hard. By now you would think I would be used to it, but I always hope each new baby will be healthy . . ."

Marie patted her hand sympathetically.

"The one thing I have learned is that God gives me enough grace for each day. He helps me just to do the next thing, day after day," Sara went on.

"I can't understand why God lets this happen to you over and over," Marie said. "And here I am having one healthy child after another. It almost makes me feel guilty."

"You don't need to feel that way! I don't understand either, but I have to believe that God's ways are higher than mine. I just have to believe that God knows best."

Sara shook her head and resolutely changed the subject. It would soon be time to go home for supper.

• • • • • • • • • •

Spring brought Sara's favorite kind of weather. She enjoyed starting her tomato plants inside and then setting them out in the freshly-plowed garden. She delighted in the outdoors. With the older children in school, she also found time to help neighbors move or paint or get ready for hosting church or whatever needed to be done. Five-year-old Verda tagged along, always a ready helper.

As a special treat Noah took the children to the Ohio Caverns in April. Cleaning the attic in solitude gave Sara the time she needed to think through her life again.

"Bless the LORD, O my soul: and all that is within me, bless his holy name" (Psalm 103:1). Sara meditated as she scrubbed and organized. Psalm 103 was one of her favorites. *"Bless the LORD, O my soul, and forget not all his benefits: who forgiveth all thine iniquities; who healeth all thy diseases; who redeemeth thy life from destruction; who crowneth thee with lovingkindness and*

tender mercies" (verses 2–4). How she cherished the mercy of God! Over and over she had claimed those promises and found balm for her heartaches. God was her loving Father. He knew how weak and frail she often felt. He forgave her shortcomings. *"For as the heaven is high above the earth, so great is his mercy toward them that fear him. As far as the east is from the west, so far hath he removed our transgressions from us. Like as a father pitieth his children, so the LORD pitieth them that fear him. For he knoweth our frame; he remembereth that we are dust"* (verses 11–14). Quietly Sara recommitted herself to God and to her family. "I need special wisdom as our children grow through their teenage years. Help me teach them to trust you for their lives. You know the future. Please help me in the days ahead."

Early in May the summer busyness began. Noah's parents came back from Florida, so Noah and Sara moved into the small house again. The children were released from school, and farming became a full-time occupation for them all. As Noah and Marvin worked in the fields, Sara, Mary Lou, Judy, and Verda tended the garden. They froze and canned scores of quarts of vegetables for the winter.

• • • • • • • • •

"Sara, I've been thinking about church." Noah found Sara working by herself and broached the difficult topic.

Sara looked up from her mending at Noah's words. She had been dreading this conversation.

"You know how so many of our friends have gone over to the neighboring church recently."

"Yes." Sara kept her needle moving dutifully.

"It seems the people there are enthusiastic about mission work. I think it would be good for the children to grow up there. They would enjoy the youth group. I hear they have Bible studies and prayer meetings . . ."

"I know." Sara spoke slowly. "My friends have been telling me that too. It's just . . . just so hard to leave the setting I grew up in. It's easier for you because your family has been going to the Conservative Mennonite church for years."

"It's not like I'm asking you to change everything. You can keep on dressing the same if you want. But I want to go over there next Sunday." Noah's voice was firm. Sara knew the decision had been made.

As Noah left the room, a single tear dropped on Sara's mending. "Lord," Sara whispered, "help me to be submissive to Noah in this. I know you have made him the leader in our home." Although they didn't always agree, she had grown to trust his judgment through the years. She hoped her sisters would understand.

To fourteen-year-old Marvin, the reasons for the church change seemed insignificant. But he got excited when Noah brought home their first car—a '41 Chevy. "I'm gonna drive it!" he said.

"First of all we practice," Noah told him. An empty field proved the perfect training ground. Together father and son learned how to handle their new conveyance.

* * * * * * * * * *

The rest of 1953 went by fairly quietly. Noah started driving a school bus for extra income. The Beachy house often brimmed over with company—friends for a meal, or relatives overnight. Sara loved to cook and, with the help of her daughters, always spread an ample table. The family visited relatives in Indiana several times.

One special weekend Sara's brother Joni and sister Wilma brought their families on the train to visit. The adults left Mary Lou and Judy in charge of the younger children while they went fishing on Lake Erie. What fun they had! The fish bit so well that Joni finally told his wife Mary, "You have to learn to bait your own hook, or I'll never get to catch any fish myself!" The laughter and sunshine, with lots of fish to fry later, made it a memorable day.

That fall Noah and his dad added a garage onto the small house where Noah, Sara, and their family lived during the summer months.

On November 4, Noah's grandfather, Amish bishop Cornelius Beachy, died at the age of ninety-one. He was a Plain City pioneer, having helped start the Amish settlement there in 1900. Melvin Mullet and Emmanuel Mullet preached the sermons at his funeral, recognizing his long and fruitful life, and encouraging his descendants to be faithful to God.

· · · · · · · · · ·

David Jay came into the world on November 20, 1954. Once again everything seemed normal. However, one doctor scribbled a warning note on the baby's chart: "Watch vital signs in baby, and if any cyanosis develops, put in incubator."

The medical personnel watched carefully, but nothing happened. What joy Sara felt as she cradled a baby in her arms once again! Her arms had ached with emptiness for too long. Sara smiled as she watched him chew on his fingers vigorously. Verna again lent her capable help as a *maud,* and the rest of the family pitched in gladly as they adapted to life with a newborn. Sara still hesitated, though. *Dare I hope again?*

Chapter 4

"He's so cute!"

Mary Lou, Judy, and Verda *oohed* and *aahed* over seven-month-old David. He was going to Aunt Lena's wedding, and in celebration of the occasion he had graduated from the traditional Amish baby dress to his first pair of pants. Marvin didn't say much, but Sara could tell from the glint in his eye and the camera in his hand how proud he was of this baby brother. Tears welled in her eyes as she thought of the happiness David had brought into their home. He was so marvelously healthy! At two months of age he had had a case of whooping cough, but since then he had thrived.

What a gorgeous June day! Large vases of peonies adorned each window in the rambling farmhouse as

Lena Beachy became Norman Yutzy's bride. Lena was the last of Eli C.'s children to marry. Eli squeezed Mary Ann's hand as they witnessed the solemn occasion.

Sara smiled as she watched her in-laws. They were always so kind and affectionate to each other. *How does it feel to have all your children grown?* she wondered. *They tried hard to raise them right.* Sara couldn't foresee that eventually four sons and two sons-in-law of Eli's would become ministers.

• • • • • • • • •

RING! RING! RING!

The insistent clanging of the telephone jarred Noah from a sound sleep.

"Hello?"

"Noah? I'm afraid I have bad news for you. There's been a house fire at Simon Slabaugh's place. Three of his sons lost their lives. Susie and the other children are in shock, but okay. Would you please drive over and break the news to their son Omer and Marie?"

"Oh, no!" Noah breathed. "Of course we'll tell them. Then we'll all start out for Indiana right away."

Sara looked questioningly at Noah as he hung up

the phone. "What happened?" she asked, wide-eyed.

As he explained, Sara began crying. "Poor Susie! Oh, my dear sister. Let's get out there as quickly as we can!"

As Noah dressed, they planned. He would drive over and tell Omer what had happened. Omer's sister Barbara was staying at Omer's house and would also hear the news. Sara would pack and make arrangements for the children to come out the next day. Marvin was out of school now. He could handle things on the farm.

When the two families arrived in Nappanee, they stopped first at Sara's sister Wilma's place to change clothes. As hugs were exchanged, Omer and Barbara learned the full story from their uncle. They had lost three brothers, aged ten, nine, and five. Their dad Simon was also among the victims. Their mouths gaped in shock. "What? How could this happen?"

"Well, it was really windy yesterday, with blowing rain and some snow. It was unusually cold for the first of November. So they started a fire in the heating stove in the big west room and somehow during the night it got out of control. Your dad had escaped with Susie and some of the children, but when he heard the screams of Glenn, Simon Jr., and Larry, he felt compelled to go back and try to rescue them. It was just too hot, and he didn't make it. I'm so sorry!"

As tears flowed, the story continued. "Martha and John Henry rushed around and found a ladder to try to reach those upstairs bedrooms, but they couldn't do it either. I'm so sorry!"

"Let's go over there right away!"

Tearfully Noah and the family drove out to view the tragic scene. The fire was still smoldering. Bluish flames marked where the bodies of the four victims still lay.

"AMISH FATHER AND THREE OF HIS THIRTEEN CHILDREN PERISH IN FARM FIRE" the headline of the November 2, 1955, *Goshen News* blazoned. Hundreds of friends, relatives, and church members flocked to help with the cleanup and comforting. The sorrow was indescribable. Sara's tears mingled with Susie's as they embraced. So often Susie had comforted Sara. Now their roles were reversed.

"We just can't always understand the way God works," Sara counseled. "Go ahead and cry, but keep trusting. God does still care about you. You will feel it later on."

· · · · · · · · ·

Life went on.

Paul Allen was born on blustery January 12, 1956. He weighed 9 pounds, 12 ounces, and his heart rate and rhythm seemed to be normal. Still the doctors were cautious. They wrote in his records, "Six brothers and sisters have died of von Gierke disease (glycogen storage of the heart). This baby will be watched carefully."

What a fussy baby! Paul cried most of his first night at home. That was only the beginning. His continual fussing concerned Sara.

"Noah, I think we should take Paul to the hospital and get his heart checked out. It just isn't normal for babies to cry this much!"

So they took Paul to the hospital to have his heart tested. The tests showed no abnormalities, and eventually he grew out of the fussy stage.

As Paul started to smile and captivate his parents' hearts, life took on new meaning for Noah and Sara. They grieved with their friends, Monroe and Lizzie Ann Kurtz, when they had a second stillborn son that February. Seeing him buried so close to the Beachy babies made Noah and Sara realize anew how precious their six healthy children were.

Sara also enjoyed watching her children's individual personalities develop. Marvin was almost grown up. His first job, siding houses with his uncle Mark Hostetler, was teaching him lots of new skills. In his time off, Marvin enjoyed keeping his Studebaker Starlight Coupe spit-polished. Mary Lou and Judy were becoming vibrant young ladies, always surrounded by friends. Now Noah and Sara often found their house occupied by giggling girls for a slumber party or a youth group for a social. Verda was stuck in the middle, six years younger than Judy, but six years older than David. She was sent on all sorts of errands, teased by the older ones, and often partially responsible for the little boys. Her sisters often said Verda didn't play with her toys—she only rearranged them. A spunky girl, she knew how to hold her own in a squabble.

"*Bless the LORD, all his works in all places of his dominion: bless the LORD, O my soul*" (Psalm 103:22). Sara's meditations these days were happy ones. *Dear God, thank you for this wonderful, precious family. You have been so faithful in blessing us! Help me to treasure each moment with them and to raise them to serve you.*

Chapter 4

"Here's a blond one!"

Sara smiled at her husband from her hospital bed in familiar Room 55. This had been her room for the last three children. How many happy memories it held! "This one is Noah, Jr., I think!"

"Well, I guess if you insist . . ." Noah hesitated. Sara had suggested that name before, but they wondered if this might be their last chance to use it. Noah wrote the name on the birth certificate. The older children were waiting in the car to take home this small baby born on April 5, 1957. The birth certificate was the last formality to complete.

"Excuse me." Their old friend Margaret Karrer looked up from her nursing chart. "I know this is none of my business, but think about that child's future. There are so many Amish and Mennonite boys named Junior! He will get everyone else's mail and have all kinds of trouble. Can't you think of a more original name?" The nurse's face flushed at her own boldness, but she felt strongly about this issue.

"You do have a point there," Noah said. "What do you think, Sara?"

"Well, I guess I'll leave it up to you and the older children. If you can think of a name that suits everyone, I guess it's okay with me. But I would like a 'Junior' too."

Noah went out to the parking lot and held a quick family conference. They settled on "Robert Gene." Since there was another Robert in church, this baby was soon called Gene.

Gene was slightly blue at birth, so the hospital staff had whisked him into an incubator and provided extra oxygen. Soon his color became normal. When he went home from the hospital two days later, he appeared to be in excellent health.

· · · · · · · · ·

"Wow, boys sure are different from girls," Sara told

her sisters. She shook her head ruefully. "What one doesn't think of, the others do. These three boys are busy from morning till night!"

"What have they been up to now?"

"Well, for example, just look at that track on the floor!" Sara pointed to a dark circle that went all the way through the kitchen, dining room, and living room. "They constantly run through these rooms with their toy tractors, cars, and even pushing chairs, chasing each other and laughing and screaming. I hope the folks won't be upset when they get home from Florida and see this!

"And I am getting a little suspicious about the number of Matchbox cars that get left in the driveway just exactly where the milk truck comes through. Then the boys want our sympathy for the squished cars and beg for new ones."

But although she sounded exasperated, Sara did not really mind. She had been longing for the noise and activity of young boys ever since baby Henry had died eleven years earlier. *I remember telling Noah that I hoped people would not pray that we have more children. Now I am thankful that God knows best. What would I do without my three little boys?*

Sara and the children especially enjoyed those winters in Dawdy Beachys' big house. There were plenty of bedrooms on the second floor, and the banisters flanking the large stairway were great for sliding and jumping. The clothes chute from the upper level saved her many steps, and the boys frequently used it for toy transport. Sara couldn't imagine what shenanigans would ensue when the boys grew tall enough to notice the transom windows above the wide doorways. For the girls, the attic was a treasure trove they loved to explore when Noah and Sara weren't around. They were fascinated by Grandma Mary Ann's fancy old dresses and other memorabilia of bygone days.

Father in heaven, I am so thankful, Sara often prayed. *Thank you for these seven healthy children! We still don't have much money, and we can't buy expensive toys or lots of new clothes, but the children are happy. They have vivid imaginations and lots of fun playing together. Thank you for these special moments today.*

• • • • • • • • •

Two years later, on January 29, 1959, LaVern joined the family. This time Marvin wasn't at home to celebrate. He had gone to a six-week Bible School. As Noah and Sara brought the baby home, Sara marveled anew at the miracle of life. After losing six babies, she now enjoyed their four healthy little boys!

In May, Marvin, Mary Lou, and Judy decided to go to their church youth meetings in Iowa. Their only hesitation about going was that LaVern was still suffering from a cold that had already hung on for two weeks. The fear that had been hidden and almost forgotten for so long came back full force. What if something happened to LaVern while they were gone?

"What do you think, Mom? Should we go or not?" Marvin asked.

"I think you should just go. It will be a good experience for you," Sara said. "We'll take care of LaVern the best we can. I don't know what to expect with him. You can call home every day to see how he is."

Marvin breathed a sigh of relief. This trip was especially important to him because he was picking up Amy Miller in Goshen, Indiana, and taking her along to the meetings. They had been writing to each other since Bible School. How eagerly he had anticipated spending the whole weekend with her! Her friendly personality, sparkling brown eyes, and sensitivity to others made her a joy to be around.

The young people found the meetings exciting and inspirational. Amy wanted to introduce Marvin to some of her relatives in Kalona, and Mary Lou and Judy soon found friends to socialize with between services. On Friday evening Marvin and Amy went to her uncle Chester Miller's house for supper. When they rejoined the youth group, they found Mary Lou and Judy in tears. "What's wrong?" they asked, immediately concerned.

"LaVern is in the hospital," Judy informed them. "He had trouble breathing, and they took him in this morning. I just know he's going to die," she went on tearfully. "It seems the children always do if they get sick enough to go to the hospital."

"I'm afraid of that too," Mary Lou said. "How soon can we leave for home, Marvin?"

"Get your things together after the meeting tonight. We'll sleep a couple of hours and then take off."

Meanwhile Noah and Sara were keeping watch at LaVern's hospital bed. They knew the latest X-rays had shown a grossly enlarged heart. The doctors said he was in "moderately severe" cardiac failure. It was only a matter of time.

The older children arrived Saturday afternoon. Grimly, they gathered around the hospital bed and said their farewells to their littlest brother.

When LaVern died at 3:00 on Sunday afternoon, Sara sighed and bit her lip to hold back her cry of anguish. It had been six years since Wilma's death, and she had almost started taking healthy babies for granted. Now chubby LaVern was gone. From deep within, the tears came.

An autopsy report didn't answer many questions. The glycogen storage disease assumed to cause the deaths of the earlier babies wasn't evident at all. Now the doctors were suggesting "endocardial fibroelastosis," saying the enlargement of the heart was caused by excessive growth of fibrous tissues. It was a rare condition, and there was no known cure.

Why can't the doctors do something to help? Sara agonized inwardly. *They've just watched my children die and can't seem to solve the problem at all. It's frustrating! But God has all power and knows all things. He knows why we have to go through this again.* An old song by W. B. Stevens came to Sara's mind. She sang it softly:

Tempted and tried, we're oft made to wonder

Why it should be thus all the day long;
While there are others living about us,
Never molested, though in the wrong.

Farther along we'll know all about it,
Farther along we'll understand why;
Cheer up, my brother, live in the sunshine,
We'll understand it all by and by.

Often when death has taken our loved ones,
Leaving our home so lone and so drear,
Then do we wonder why others prosper,
Living so wicked year after year.

Soon we will see our dear, loving Savior,
Hear the last trumpet sound through the sky;
Then we will meet those gone on before us,
Then we shall know and understand why.[1]

"Farther along . . ." How hard it seemed to Sara to have to wait to understand all about it! Only her solid faith in a God who cared and an eternity of reward ahead kept her going day after day.

Once again the dreary business of preparing for a

---

[1] Public domain.

funeral began, and the sickly sweet smell of embalming chemicals filled the house. Sara pulled a piece of soft white fabric from her cupboard and asked two young girls, Mary Troyer and Sarah Gingerich, to make the funeral dress. They wanted to help, but this made death so real and personal to them that it was a very difficult task. "Now we can understand a bit more what Mary Lou and Judy have had to go through six times already!" they whispered to each other. "How can they take it so well?"

When the body was dressed, the family solemnly gathered together in the front room. In the small casket they saw a tiny body reposing peacefully in a simple white dress. "He looks just like an angel," Marvin said.

The *Plain City Advocate* printed the following on the front page of the May 13 edition:

PLAIN CITY BABY, LAVERN BEACHY, DIED SUNDAY

LaVern Beachy, age 3 months, of Plain City RFD 1, died Sunday at Children's Hospital in Columbus. Survived by parents, Mr. and Mrs. Noah E. Beachy, 3 sisters, Mary Lou, Judith Ann and Verda; 4 brothers, Marvin, David,

Paul and Robert Gene, all at home. Funeral services were held at 9 a.m. Wednesday, May 13, at the home of the parents, the Rev. Eldon Troyer and the Rev. Raymond Kauffman officiating. Interment in Canaan Amish Mennonite Cemetery by Charles Jay Ferguson.

The house was crowded for the funeral. Marvin's friend Amy had asked Uncle Joni Hochstetler about a ride out from Goshen, and came with some of Marvin's cousins. Just before the funeral, she met Noah and the surprisingly young-looking Sara for the first time. Taking her place beside Marvin, Amy self-consciously joined the family for the service.

For the little Beachy boys, this funeral was a new experience, and they didn't know exactly what to expect. Instinctively they sensed the solemnity. They were very quiet.

Going to the graveyard was the most difficult part for Sara this time. In direct contrast to the springtime season of new life bursting forth, they were laying away another precious, lifeless baby.

There were two rows of babies in the cemetery by now: seven of theirs, three stillborn children of Monroe and Lizzie Ann Kurtz, and several others from their church. This new grave would not have a stone either. They simply could not afford one. As tears rolled down her cheeks, Sara suddenly felt old—old and very tired. In silence she poured out her heart to God. *Oh, Lord, this sorrow . . . it just doesn't get any easier. Hold me closer, Lord. You are my refuge and my strength. The only way I can walk through this valley of shadow again is with you.*

Chapter 14

"She said yes!"

Marvin's joyful announcement brought a cheer from his sisters. Amy had consented to marry Marvin during his weekend visit to Indiana in November.

"Well, we're real happy for you," Noah spoke for himself and Sara. "Marriage is a big responsibility for you—being just twenty—but it is also a joy. You've picked a real nice girl. I'm sure you'll be happy."

Marvin nodded his head in agreement. "One downside is that we'll be living in Indiana, but that's not too far away. I think we'll move a house trailer up close to her folks. It seems like there are plenty of construction jobs out there, so it should be easy to get work."

"We'll miss you," Sara said quietly.

• • • • • • • • •

That winter Noah and Sara took Verda, David, Paul, and Gene to Sarasota, Florida, to visit Dawdy Beachys. It was a big adventure for all of them, highlighted by seeing wild hogs and riding a work horse at Myakka River State Park. The latter was especially memorable because Verda, the boys, and a stranger all rode the horse at once. The ride went smoothly, but when they dismounted, the stranger ended up in the water trough!

In January, Marvin moved to Indiana to start his new job. Without the help of his oldest son, Noah found the chores noticeably heavier, and Mary Lou and Judy had to pitch in. Even Rex, their German shepherd/collie mix, didn't cooperate as well with Marvin gone. Marvin had trained the dog to get the cows on his own without human supervision. But try as he might, Noah could not make that dog fetch the cows. So he had to get them himself.

Paul also had a special friendship with Rex. The two would go out "rabbit-hunting" by the hour, even though Paul was too young to take a gun along. One day they were gone so long that the family grew concerned. It was almost dark. Where were they? Only when Noah climbed up in the barn and looked out a hayloft window did he see the two scampering in the woods. When the anxious father reached his son, Paul nonchalantly explained, "We were having fun running the rabbits."

With spring came the bustle of preparing for Marvin's wedding. Each of the girls had a new dress—yellow for Verda, pink for Judy, and green for Mary Lou. Sara made a dark blue one for herself. Sewing was a task she didn't really enjoy, but she had learned through necessity to sew quickly and neatly.

It was a Friday evening when they arrived in Goshen. "So are you all ready for the big day?" Noah asked his son.

"As ready as we can be, just a bit nervous. Come on out and look at our little home," Marvin invited. The mobile home was set up next door to Amy's folks and they were ready to move in.

"This china is so pretty," Sara told Amy as she carefully helped her wash and arrange the new dishes.

"Yes, I love the gray rose design. It will be so much fun to use. Thanks for helping me put it in the cupboards!"

Marvin and Amy's simple wedding ceremony was

held at Pleasant Grove Conservative Mennonite Church on Sunday, April 10, 1960. Sara cuddled the sleeping Gene while Noah kept David and Paul sitting quietly on the hard wooden benches. Sara's thoughts wandered freely in the solemn afternoon quietness. *What a beautiful service! I'm glad the sun is shining! Amy looks so pretty in light blue.* A few tears of happiness blurred the lovely scene. *Ah, my strong, handsome, oldest son! He looks so grown up in that suit. What a joy he's been to us! It does seem he's plenty young to get married. We even had to sign for his marriage license. But I guess Noah was even younger. I'm just so thankful that Marvin is serving God and has picked a godly companion. I sure hope they won't need to go through as many rough times as we have, but we'll trust the future to God.* Sara could never have guessed the future of service God had in store for her son, who would become the founder of the Gospel Echoes Team Prison Ministry.

• • • • • • • • • •

Exactly a year later Marvin and Amy brought Catherine Rose home from the hospital. "How does it feel to be a grandpa at forty-one?" Marvin asked when he called his dad.

"It feels pretty good!" Noah said. "Is everything okay?"

"Everyone's fine! The baby's got lots of dark hair and big blue eyes. You'll have to come see her."

And they did! Right away the new grandma and grandpa brought out Aunt Mary Lou to help with the baby. Then every month after that, it seemed they either traveled to Goshen, or Marvin and Amy came to Plain City. Noah and Sara were seriously thinking about moving to Indiana, so they also went farm-hunting frequently. *It would be so nice if we could live near my family, as well as our son and our new grandbaby.* Sara's brown eyes sparkled at the thought. *I don't want to miss watching every stage as she grows up.*

Chapter 14

"But I'm a grandmother!"

Sara felt a bit overwhelmed when she discovered she was expecting another child. Somehow she had assumed LaVern would be the last. This time she couldn't seem to shake off her weariness. One flight of stairs could leave her breathless.

Finally in September, Dr. Karrer insisted that Sara enter the University Hospital in Columbus. "I don't like the sound of your heartbeat, and you tire too easily. And your ankles have been swelling too much. I want you to get a thorough checkup."

So Sara went to the hospital. She didn't have to worry much about things at home since the older girls ran the household capably. Only Verda and David were in school, and the younger boys were old enough to no longer need constant attention.

For three weeks Sara went through various tests. Doctors removed a small piece of heart muscle to see if she might have adult glycogen storage disease, but she didn't. They took an electrocardiogram and gave her a cardiac fluoroscopy.

"Sara, we have your test results." Dr. Ryan stood beside the hospital bed on the last day of September. Thoughtfully, he tapped his pen against the clipboard. "We really don't have any answers for you. It is obvious you have some sort of heart disease, but it's not fitting a specific diagnosis. We're going to send you home, but you have to take it easy. I know you have a big family and lots to do, but you are not healthy. Please rest as much as you can for your sake and for the baby. We'll see you back here in December."

Dr. Ryan's letter to Dr. Karrer had much more specific instructions:

> *Dear Doctor Karrer:*
> *This is just a follow-up note to our conversation regarding Mrs. Beachy. That she was in cardiac failure was quite apparent, but as I said*

previously, I have no idea what kind of heart disease she has. I am sure it must be related to the fact that she has had seven children [with] supposed glycogen storage disease. The only thing we came up with was the physical findings and symptomology of heart failure as you did with gallop rhythm and tachycardia. She had left bundle branch block on her electrocardiograms. She seemed to be approximately 4½ months pregnant. Her admission weight was 138 pounds, and her weight at discharge was 130 . . . She seemed to be improved at the time of discharge, but for the three weeks she was here she was very inactive. As I said over the phone, she walked out in the hall one evening and [had] a little nocturnal dyspnea that night. She wished to go home, and I can't say as I blame her. We discharged her to you on digoxin 1/4 mg b.i.d., hydrochlorothiazide 50 mg b.i.d., and a 2 gr sodium diet. You may have to add mercurate at whatever interval you think necessary to keep her at a steady dry weight. After our telephone conversation, I spoke with Dr. Copeland, and he would be only too happy to deliver Mrs. Beachy at term. We should see her in about 2 weeks, I think. As I said, she may have to spend the last month in the hospital. I am not sure that she realizes how sick she is, and I don't believe that her husband as yet appreciates this fact. She should be quite inactive around home now because the load of pregnancy begins to pick up, reaching its peak at about three weeks only to return at the time of labor.

We certainly enjoyed seeing and taking care of this very pleasant and very interesting lady. I wish we had an answer as to what type of heart disease this is. Feel free to call us at any time.

Best regards,
Joseph M. Ryan, M.D.

That fall Noah and Sara found a farm to rent near Emmatown, Indiana. Sara was excited because this would mean living close to her brother Jerome as well as to her mother, who had married Levi Mast and moved to that area. Noah and Sara planned to move in January. Hopefully in a year or two they would then be able to buy a farm out there.

"January?" Judy wailed. "How can we move in

January? Andy and I want to get married in April!"

"That's easy, Judy," Noah told her. "Just move out with us, have the wedding out there, and then move back."

"Da-a-a-d! I don't want to do that! All our friends are here. His family all live around here, and we don't know what the church will be like in Indiana! Besides, I have to be here to get our house trailer ready!"

"Judy, maybe you could move your wedding date up and get married here before we move," Sara suggested.

"We'll talk about it," Judy said.

"But remember," Noah said firmly, "your mother will need help with this move. No matter when the wedding is, we'll be expecting your help when we move."

"Okay, Dad."

• • • • • • • • • •

On December 12, 1961, Sara was admitted to the hospital to wait for the new baby's arrival. It was hard to lie there day after day, knowing that Judy was preparing for her wedding (now slated for January) and Noah was preparing for the move. At least the cows had been sold, so the chores were easier. To make the time go faster, Sara worked on a piece of embroidery for her granddaughter. The pastel figures and cross-stitch letters of "Now I lay me down to sleep . . ." soon filled the canvas as she stitched day by day.

Sara often used her enforced resting time to commune with God. *Lord, what are you trying to teach me this time? I need your strength for all the changes ahead! Would you please take care of this new baby? And help us to get everything done that needs to be done for the move and the wedding. Help Noah especially to have patience and wisdom with his responsibilities. Help Judy and Andy as they get ready to start their life together. May they keep you as the center of their home. Help all our children to follow you faithfully all their lives. Please do not let them be bitter because they lost so many siblings and we were so desperately poor. Help them to remember the many times you provided for us in miraculous ways and the love that people showed us. Give them victory in each struggle . . .*

Leaving her cares in the heavenly Father's capable hands, Sara relaxed. Each time the family came to visit, they found a cheerful, encouraging mother who was still very much the heart of their home.

Finally, on December 24, Sharon Sue was born. The family instantly fell in love with the fragile-looking baby—their Christmas bundle. Marvin and his family came out again to share the holidays. Even though Sara and the baby were in the hospital, it was a festive time.

At two days of age, Sharon Sue had several cyanotic episodes where her lips and fingernails turned markedly blue. Reluctantly the family transferred the baby to Children's Hospital for treatment. There, X-rays revealed that the little girl's heart was already enlarged, but a muscle biopsy did not show glycogen storage disease. Doctors kept her in the hospital for eleven days, but reached no conclusion. A frustrated doctor scrawled on her chart: "The nature of the heart disease is still undiagnosed, but is probably not glycogenosis. 'Idiopathic cardiomyopathy,' whatever that is, is a remote possibility."

Sharon Sue came home to a house full of escalating busyness. Judy was sewing for the wedding, and Mary Lou was finishing up her job in town. Then the girls and Sara packed belongings and housecleaned while Noah cleaned the shop and attended to business details. On January 6 there was company to celebrate Old Christmas (Epiphany) and to see the baby. A group of neighbors brought ice cream and cake along with a gift of lawn chairs and a porch swing for a surprise farewell. Their kindness touched Noah and Sara. How they would miss these friends!

On Wednesday, January 17, Marvin and Amy brought some relatives to help prepare for the wedding and the move. Somehow in between the work, Sara found time to write descriptive diary entries:

> *January 17, 1962, Wednesday: Had a lot of help. Baked sheet cakes. Marvins, Susie, Sylvia, and Barbara came for dinner. Potatoes were cooked in jackets. Ironing was finished. It was a cold day. Noah, Marvin, and Omer took a load of furniture to Indiana. Came back a little late that evening.*
>
> *January 18, 1962, Thursday: Had plenty of help. Cooked potatoes. Baked a few cakes yet. Frosted all sheet cakes. Noah and Marvin and I went to Columbus to get plates, cups, napkins, ice cream, and all things for the wedding. Sharon was brauf [well-behaved]. It was cold! Floors scrubbed and porches. Got Christena in Columbus at 4:30 in the morning at airport. Wayne came along.*
>
> *January 19, 1962, Friday: Had plenty of help. Made sloppy joe (28 pounds). Cooked tapioca for pudding. Finished the wedding cake. Cleaned*

the rest of the house. Set up wedding tables and set them. Had plenty of help. Also cut up celery and cooked eggs.

January 20, 1962, Saturday: Judith and Andrew Gingerich married today. The sun shone and there were snow flurries part time. Was a beautiful day! Pretty cold. Had close to 300 for dinner. They received a nice variety of gifts. In the evening there were between 50 and 70 people for supper. Everything was pretty well guessed in eats. Some potato salad and cake left. Joe Dans had Sharon Sue.

Sara clipped the article about Judy's wedding from the January 24 edition of the *Plain City Advocate* and tucked it into her diary.

BEACHY-GINGERICH VOWS SPOKEN
On Saturday, Jan. 20, at the Canaan Amish Mennonite Church, Bishop Steve Yoder of Nappanee, Ind., officiated at the marriage of Miss Judith Beachy, daughter of Mr. and Mrs. Noah E. Beachy, and Mr. Andrew Gingerich,

son of Mr. and Mrs. Jonas Gingerich. The attendants were Miss Mary Lou Beachy, sister of the bride, Mr. Ervin Troyer, and Mr. and Mrs. Lester Gingerich. A reception for between two and three hundred from Ohio, Indiana, and Florida was held at the home of the bride's parents. The young couple will live in a house-trailer near the home of the groom's parents. Mr. Gingerich is employed at the Dobb's-Evans Paper Company in Columbus. Mr. and Mrs. Noah E. Beachy and family moved this week to Emmatown, Indiana, where he will be engaged in farming.

Sara closed her diary with a sigh and got the rocker moving with a push of her foot. *A daughter married! I can hardly believe how quickly my children are growing up! I am so thankful everything went well today, but I sure am tired!* She smiled at tiny Sharon Sue drifting off to sleep for the night in her arms. *What does God have in mind for this little one?* "You are such a precious sweetheart!" Sara murmured in her ear. "I will treasure every day I have with you." Sara kissed her soft forehead and laid her gently in the bassinet.

Chapter

"Susie, I need a favor."

Sara looked at her sister, busy cleaning up the aftermath of the wedding. "Would you consider taking Sharon Sue back with you to Indiana?"

"Oh, Sara, I don't know. She is so fragile. What if something happens to her while she's with me?" Susie looked anxious.

"Sharon Sue is in God's hands. If it's her time to go, she will go, whether she's with me or you," Sara said. "I'd just feel better if she wasn't in all the cold air and commotion around here."

So Susie took the baby and Sara concentrated on the move. With lots of help, including Judy's, Noah and the family moved to Indiana on Tuesday.

Sara wrote:

January 23, 1962, Tuesday: Was cold. Moved from Ohio to Indiana. Started at 4:00, got here at 10:25. Ate dinner at Mothers. Levis and Marvins brought supper in. Everything was unloaded by 3:00. Trucks left for home [driven by] Eldon Troyer, Eli Hochstetler, Melvin Miller, and Noah Gingerich. Was cold and icy.

January 24, 1962, Wednesday: All the sisters and wives were here and brought dinner in. Helped clean and straighten up. Hung more curtains. Enjoyed the day. Susie brought Sharon along over. She was a good baby . . .

After Noah and Sara took Christena back to the Indianapolis airport, the family tried to settle into a new routine. But Sharon Sue was sick. Only six days after the move, Noah and Sara took her to Marvin's home, carrying her on a pillow to ease the baby's discomfort. "What doctor should we go to?" they asked.

Amy recommended Dr. Troyer, who immediately sent them to the Goshen General Hospital. The staff there quickly put Sharon Sue on oxygen. Although she improved at first, her frail body was not strong enough, and her heart stopped beating at 8:30 p.m. on January 29. The next day *The Goshen News* reported:

SHARON SUE BEACHY

Sharon Sue Beachy, five-week-old daughter of Mr. and Mrs. Noah Beachy, Route 1, Topeka, died about 8:30 p.m. Monday at the Goshen General Hospital. The child had been ill since birth of a heart ailment and was admitted at the hospital Monday noon.

Sharon Sue was born Dec. 24, last, at Plain City, Ohio, and moved with her parents to the Topeka community about a week ago. Surviving, in addition to the parents, are four brothers, Marvin Ray, Route 1 Topeka [Goshen], David, Paul and Robert, all at home; three sisters, Mrs. Andrew (Judith) Gingerich, Plain City, Ohio, and Mary Lou and Verda, both at home; and the grandparents, Mr. and Mrs. Eli C. Beachy, Plain City, Ohio, and Mrs. Levi Mast, Route 1, Topeka.

> Friends will be received after 7 p.m. today at the family home near Emmatown. Funeral services will be held Wednesday at 1:30 p.m. at the Fair Haven Conservative [Amish] Mennonite Church, east of Goshen, with burial in the nearby cemetery. Bishop David Bontrager will officiate. The Miller-Yoder Funeral Home at Middlebury is in charge of arrangements.

Sadly Sara caressed the lifeless body of her last baby. Exactly three years ago LaVern had been born, and he was no longer with them either. Her heart wept.

Ladies from the Fair Haven Church made a dress and head covering for the tiny baby. The young folks came and sang at the house. On Noah's forty-second birthday, they buried Sharon Sue in a cold, windy graveyard two hundred miles away from the graves of her brothers and sisters back in Plain City. Holding back tears, the young folks sang the familiar Fanny Crosby hymn:

> Safe in the arms of Jesus,
> Safe on His gentle breast
> There by his love o'ershaded,
> Sweetly my soul shall rest.

Hark 'tis the voice of angels,
Borne in a song to me,
Over the fields of glory,
Over the jasper sea.

Safe in the arms of Jesus,
Safe on His gentle breast,
There by his love o'ershaded,
Sweetly my soul shall rest.[1]

It was over.

* * * * * * * * * *

"*Safe in the arms of Jesus . . .*" The words kept repeating themselves in Sara's mind one morning as she sat in her rocker for a quiet time before the three little boys started their day. *Oh, dear God, thank you that our darling Sharon Sue is safe with you. It has been such a long journey these last fifteen years. I do not understand why we had to lose so many babies.* Sara rested her chin on her cupped hand and let the tears flow. The pain still

---

[1] Public domain.

lingered, not sharp and biting as it had been at first, but tender with all those unfulfilled dreams. Sharon Sue. LaVern. Wilma. Miriam. Howard. William. Barbara Jean. Henry.

For nine months Sara had carried each precious life through the joys and discomforts of pregnancy. She had waited and feared and prayed. She had labored and agonized to bring each baby into the world. Then she had been permitted only a few months to care for them and love them before they were snatched out of her arms. Like a candle flame, their lives had been snuffed out in a moment, and they were gone.

Lord, I don't understand why so many of our children had to die as tiny babies. I still miss them! Oh, God, I still have no answers. I don't know why you chose this path for me, for us. But I do accept it, Father. I do believe that your ways are higher than mine. I believe that 'farther along we'll know all about it.' I trust you! Through my tears, I trust you. Once more I lay my grief before you. Thank you that you understand how frail I am. Thank you that you don't scold me for my tears and questions. You have so faithfully taken care of us and given me strength day by day.

Sara picked up her Bible and opened it to the Psalms.

The worn pages were marked with notes and underlines. How these words had ministered to her over and over! "Bless the LORD, O my soul: and all that is within me, bless his holy name. Bless the LORD, O my soul, and forget not all his benefits" (103:1–2). Memories flooded her mind of all the ways people had helped them through the years. All the gifts of money and food and clothes. All the letters and visits and hours of working together. God had been faithful! He had given them so many benefits!

"Who forgiveth all thine iniquities; who healeth all thy diseases; who redeemeth thy life from destruction; who crowneth thee with lovingkindness and tender mercies; who satisfieth thy mouth with good things; so that thy youth is renewed like the eagle's" (Psalm 103:3–5).

Sara closed her eyes and lifted her hands. *O God, I give my life again to you. I believe you will redeem these years that look to us like destruction. I trust your lovingkindness and your tender mercies. You have blessed us with seven healthy children. Thank you for them—especially for these three little boys.* Sara had to smile a bit. Already she could hear rustlings upstairs. This quiet time wouldn't last much longer. *When I thought I couldn't bear the risk of having more children, you blessed us with these. We need so much wisdom in training them!*

Sara went back to reading Psalm 103. "The LORD is merciful and gracious, slow to anger, and plenteous in mercy. . . . He hath not dealt with us after our sins; nor rewarded us according to our iniquities. For as the heaven is high above the earth, so great is his mercy toward them that fear him" (8, 10–11).

Father, when I think of how I sinned against you as a teenager, I just thank you for salvation. Thank you for forgiveness. Thank you that even though Noah and I failed so many times, you always forgave us and helped us start over. And now you have given us a brand new start here in Indiana. Thank you for that, Father.

"But the mercy of the LORD is from everlasting to everlasting upon them that fear him, and his righteousness unto children's children" (Psalm 103:17). Sara smiled as she thought of her sweet granddaughter, Catherine Rose. The same God that had been so close and merciful to Sara through the fiery years of loss was walking ahead of the next generation. Resolutely Sara put the sorrows behind her. She would never forget, but today was a new day. Those tears had softened her heart forever, and would enable her to comfort and encourage others in the years ahead. But for now, she would choose joy. A new era of grandmother-hood beckoned ahead. New friends were to be made in Indiana. New adjustments would come, but she knew from experience that God would be faithful. She could walk into the future unafraid, cherishing each moment God gave her. God would hold her near!

Epilogue

It was in 1986 that the family purchased five gravestones to mark the resting places of the babies in the barren Plain City cemetery, and a family conversation began that led to the writing of this book.

"What was it really like to grow up in a family with all these children dying? How did it affect your lives? And how did Grandma stay so sweet?" As the oldest granddaughter, I wanted to know.

Marvin, my dad, looked around at his brothers and sisters. "I think it made me appreciate life more. I understood what was important, and that helped me decide to go into full-time prison ministry."

"And our family is unusually close because of all we went through," Mary Lou said. "We all love each other and don't have that petty fighting that divides some families."

"Mom had such a faith in God." Judy shook her head in amazement. "She was always patient, loving, and giving even while going through hardships. She was grateful for whatever we had. Mom's example of never getting bitter helped me when I went through trials as an adult."

"My experience was different from anyone else. I had to grow up so fast! No one had time to meet my needs because the three children before me and the three children after me all died." Verda looked around the circle. "Then on top of that, Mary Lou and I both became widows so young! But you know, I have learned through it all to be sensitive to the hurts of other people. I feel I can develop close relationships with them."

"What about the three 'little boys'?" I smiled at my uncles. They had been such mischievous youngsters! They were so close in age to their four oldest nieces that they had spent much of their childhood playing with them.

"I think we were spared a lot of the hurts and sorrows the older children went through," David said. "I do know I will be pretty concerned about the health of my babies. But we just have to trust the future to God. He is in control."

"Mom was a wonderful woman," Paul said. "I learned so much from her faith. And I think all my brothers and sisters are more special to me because of what we went through."

"I don't remember anything about LaVern or Sharon Sue," Gene said, "but I am looking forward to meeting all eight of my siblings in heaven. I am determined to treasure my family while I have them, and spend quality time with my children as they come along."

"Somebody should write this story," I said. "It is too important to be forgotten!"

"You should do that," Verda encouraged. "Maybe by reading our story, others will be motivated to trust God through the trials they face. They will see that God is a faithful refuge and strength. And it will remind people that family is a precious blessing!"

Someone in the circle began to sing. "Hold them near while they're here, and don't wait for tomorrow, to look back and wish for today."[1]

---

[1] "We Have This Moment Today." Words by Gloria Gaither. Music by William J. Gaither. ©Copyright 1975 by William J. Gaither. All rights reserved. Used by permission.

A Tribute to Mother

Many changes came through the years, but Noah and Sara remained faithful to the Lord. Sara died January 23, 1978. The following tribute was read at her funeral:

MEMORIAL TO MOTHER

Sara (Hochstetler) Beachy, daughter of Henry C. and Mary Hochstetler, was born July 1, 1918; went to be with Jesus on January 23, 1978, age 59 years, 6 months, and 22 days.

Married to Noah E. Beachy, March 26, 1939. Lived in matrimony 38 years, 9 months, 27 days. To this union were born 15 children. Surviving is her husband, 4 sons, and 3 daughters; Marvin, Goshen; Mrs. Larry (Mary Lou) Flowers, Ligonier; Mrs. Andrew (Judith) Gingerich, Plain City, Ohio; Mrs. Ervin (Verda) Miller, and David, both of Middlebury; Paul and Gene, both at home. Thirteen grandchildren mourn Grandma's passing.

Also surviving are 3 sisters and 1 brother; Mrs. Levi (Barbara) Troyer, Middlebury; Mrs. Crist (Christena) Bontrager, Sarasota, Florida; Jonas, Nappanee; and Mrs. Omer (Wilma) Hochstetler, Milford. Also 8 step-brothers and 3 step-sisters.

Preceding her in death were 4 sons and 4 daughters, all of whom died in their infancy of a congenital heart disease.

Mother's passing was the third in her family within the past 11 months; her mother on March 20, 1977, and a sister on December 10, 1977. Mother's heart condition worsened within the past year, and she suffered a stroke on Saturday morning, January 7, while in Sarasota, Florida. One of her sons read Psalm 23 to her, and at the end of the reading, she requested

Psalm 91. Later that morning from her hospital bed, she expressed her desire to be anointed. Bro. Lester Gingerich officiated at this service along with Harvey Miller, John F. Miller, and the family present. Her response immediately following the anointing was, "Praise the Lord!"

In the days following her stroke, Mother's mind was alert and she was able to talk with family and friends. At her request, several of the grandchildren were permitted to come up to her room and sing several songs. On January 20, she suffered a cardiac arrest. Her heart was revived again, but she never regained full consciousness and early on Monday, January 23, she went on to be with the Lord.

In November of 1978, Noah married widow Lizzie Ann Kurtz, who served as his faithful companion as the boys continued to grow up and leave home. In 1992, Lizzie Ann passed away, and Noah married Sadie Yoder in 1993. They enjoyed twelve years of matrimony before Noah's death in October 2005.

Family Record of
Noah E. Beachy & Sara (Hochstetler) Beachy

Noah was born January 31, 1920;

died October 27, 2005.

Sara was born July 1, 1918; died January 23, 1978.

Children

MARVIN RAY	October 22, 1939	
MARY LOU	December 5, 1940	
JUDITH ANN	April 25, 1942	
BARBARA JEAN	April 4, 1944	d. January 26, 1946
HENRY N.	October 5, 1945	d. January 14, 1946
WILLIAM N.	October 20, 1946	d. November 21, 1946
VERDA	January 24, 1948	
HOWARD N.	September 16, 1949	d. November 1, 1949
MIRIAM N.	November 19, 1951	d. January 9, 1952
WILMA IRENE	December 15, 1952	d. January 23, 1953
DAVID JAY	November 20, 1954	
PAUL ALLEN	January 12, 1956	
ROBERT GENE	April 5, 1957	
LAVERN N.	January 29, 1959	d. May 10, 1959
SHARON SUE	December 24, 1961	d. January 29, 1962

The Noah Beachy family around 1960.

Back row, left to right: Amy, Marvin, Noah, Sara
Middle: Judy, Verda, Mary Lou
Front: Paul, Gene, David

Medical Explanation of the Genetic Heart Defect in This Story

When Noah and Sara lost their babies, the doctors were puzzled about the cause. Dr. Annemarie Sommer from the Columbus Children's Hospital did a study on the family in 1971. The results were published in an article called "Familial Cardiomyopathy" and printed in *The Cardiovascular Series*, "Birth Defects: Original Article Series," Vol. VIII, No. 5, August, 1972.

In a personal interview with the author in 1986, Dr. Sommer expressed continued interest in the family. She also said that if those children were born today, heart transplants would probably be the only solution to the idiopathic non-obstructive cardiomyopathy they suffered from.

Since then, genetic research has uncovered the MYBPC3 mutation, and this was found in some of the surviving Beachy children. This defect disables the binding of the muscle cells of the heart, so instead of lining up for efficient pumping, the muscle cells are disorganized. The body realizes something is wrong, and produces more muscle cells to compensate. The result is severely thickened heart muscle tissue, an enlarged heart that does not pump blood effectively. This part of the condition is chronic. The secondary, acute problem is that the electrical system of the heart is also disorganized, which can lead to irregular heartbeats (arrhythmia) and even sudden cardiac arrest. The MYBPC3 mutation is passed on through autosomal dominant inheritance, which means that if both parents pass on the gene, the child will likely be affected as an infant. If only one parent passes on the gene, the child will likely be affected as a teen or young adult. Some medical treatments such as medication, surgery to correct obstructions, or implantable devices to correct heart rhythms may alleviate symptoms, but there is no cure. In severe cases, a heart transplant may be the only solution. If there is a family history of unexplained heart issues or sudden cardiac arrest, genetic testing is recommended for appropriate treatment.

Family lore traditionally ascribed all the baby deaths to "the heart problem," but the more that is learned about this genetic issue, the more likely it becomes that Barbara Jean's death was due to pneumonia instead.

ABOUT THE AUTHOR

Catherine (Beachy) Yoder lives in New Paris, Indiana, with her husband, Kenton. They have one married son, and one son and three daughters still at home. The arrival of their first grandson has ushered them into a new season of life. Homemaking is still her primary occupation.

Catherine has always loved teaching. She earned her bachelor's degree in elementary education from Grace College in 1984 and spent several years teaching at a Christian school. She then homeschooled her children at various stages. Catherine enjoyed the privilege of teaching Bible classes in the local public schools for ten years. She is also involved in her church, Salem Mennonite, and volunteer work.

Hold Them Near is her first book-length work. Personal memories of a special grandmother and a desire to preserve this story for the benefit of others were the motivation and inspiration for writing this book.

Catherine welcomes responses from her readers and invites you to email her at bookworm@bnin.net. You may also write to her in care of Christian Aid Ministries, P.O. Box 360, Berlin, Ohio 44610.

CHRISTIAN AID MINISTRIES

Christian Aid Ministries was founded in 1981 as a nonprofit, tax-exempt 501(c)(3) organization. Its primary purpose is to provide a trustworthy and efficient channel for Amish, Mennonite, and other conservative Anabaptist groups and individuals to minister to physical and spiritual needs around the world. This is in response to the command to ". . . do good unto all men, especially unto them who are of the household of faith" (Galatians 6:10).

Each year, CAM supporters provide approximately 15 million pounds of food, clothing, medicines, seeds, Bibles, Bible story books, and other Christian literature for needy people. Most of the aid goes to orphans and Christian families. Supporters' funds also help to clean up and rebuild for natural disaster victims, put up Gospel billboards in the U.S., support several church-planting efforts, operate two medical clinics, and provide resources for needy families to make their own living. CAM's main purposes for providing aid are to help and encourage God's people and bring the Gospel to a lost and dying world.

CAM has staff, warehouses, and distribution networks in Romania, Moldova, Ukraine, Haiti, Nicaragua, Liberia, Israel, and Kenya. Aside from management, supervisory personnel, and bookkeeping operations, volunteers do most of the work at CAM locations. Each year, volunteers at our warehouses, field bases, Disaster Response Services projects, and other locations donate over 200,000 hours of work.

CAM's ultimate purpose is to glorify God and help enlarge His kingdom. ". . . whatsoever ye do, do all to the glory of God" (1 Corinthians 10:31).

THE WAY TO GOD AND PEACE

We live in a world contaminated by sin. Sin is anything that goes against God's holy standards. When we do not follow the guidelines that God our Creator gave us, we are guilty of sin. Sin separates us from God, the source of life.

Since the time when the first man and woman, Adam and Eve, sinned in the Garden of Eden, sin has been universal. The Bible says that we all have "sinned and come short of the glory of God" (Romans 3:23). It also says that the natural consequence for that sin is eternal death, or punishment in an eternal hell: "Then when lust hath conceived, it bringeth forth sin: and sin, when it is finished, bringeth forth death" (James 1:15).

But we do not have to suffer eternal death in hell. God

provided forgiveness for our sins through the death of His only Son, Jesus Christ. Because Jesus was perfect and without sin, He could die in our place. "For God so loved the world that he gave his only begotten Son, that whosoever believeth in him should not perish, but have everlasting life" (John 3:16).

A sacrifice is something given to benefit someone else. It costs the giver greatly. Jesus was God's sacrifice. Jesus' death takes away the penalty of sin for everyone who accepts this sacrifice and truly repents of their sins. To repent of sins means to be truly sorry for and turn away from the things we have done that have violated God's standards (Acts 2:38; 3:19).

Jesus died, but He did not remain dead. After three days, God's Spirit miraculously raised Him to life again. God's Spirit does something similar in us. When we receive Jesus as our sacrifice and repent of our sins, our hearts are changed. We become spiritually alive! We develop new desires and attitudes (2 Corinthians 5:17). We begin to make choices that please God (1 John 3:9). If we do fail and commit sins, we can ask God for forgiveness. "If we confess our sins, he is faithful and just to forgive us our sins, and to cleanse us from all unrighteousness" (1 John 1:9).

Once our hearts have been changed, we want to continue growing spiritually. We will be happy to let Jesus be the Master of our lives and will want to become more like Him. To do this, we must meditate on God's Word and commune with God in prayer. We will testify to others of this change by being baptized and sharing the good news of God's victory over sin and death. Fellowship with a faithful group of believers will strengthen our walk with God (1 John 1:7).